BARKING UP THE RIGHT TREE

Breeding, rearing and training

the Guide Dog way

DEREK FREEMAN

RINGPRESS

RINGPRESS

Published by Ringpress Books Ltd,
Spirella House, Bridge Road,
Letchworth, Herts, SG6 4ET

Discounts available for bulk orders
Contact the Special Sales Manager at
the above address. Telephone (0462) 674177

First Published 1991
© 1991 Derek Freeman MBE

ISBN 0 948955 767

Printed and bound in Singapore
by Kyodo Printing Co

ACKNOWLEDGEMENTS

My thanks to the many people who assisted and encouraged me to write this book.

To **JULIAN OXLEY**, Director General of the Guide Dogs for the Blind Association, the GDBA senior veterinary adviser, **MR D. B. LANE**, B.Sc., FRCVS, for his help and advice.

To **NEIL EWART**, present Breeding Manager, for the GDBA, who was seconded to the project in order to extract and assemble the information on to tape – a difficult task made enjoyable by many of his novel dog training inducements to get my tongue wagging.

To **WILSON STEPHENS**, consultant to *The Field* for contributing the Foreword.

To **BIDDY BAXTER** for the use of Blue Peter photographs.

To the many **BREEDERS** who, over the years, helped me build up my knowledge of dogs.

To **SPECIALISTS** in the veterinary profession, particularly to **GARY CLAYTON JONES** B.Sc FRCVS, Director of the Royal College of Veterinary Science, Potters Bar, for his help and advice on OCD and H.D. over the years.

To **BROOD BITCH OWNERS**, **STUD DOG OWNERS**, **PUPPY WALKERS** and **GUIDE DOG OWNERS**, who all contributed to my store of information.

Most of all, to the many **PUPPIES**, **DOGS** and **BITCHES**, I have owned, trained or known throughout my life – without them there would be no book.

Dedication

To Margaret, my wife, and three daughters,
Judith, Sarah and Helen, who over many years, accepted
and educated, in our home,
dozens of canine boarders in order to help
overcome certain problems which the puppies
were undergoing during their development period.

Contents

Foreword   **6**

Introduction   **9**

PART I: GUIDE DOGS FOR THE BLIND   **13**

Chapter One: Looking Back   **14**

Chapter Two: Birth Of The Breeding Centre   **28**

Chapter Three: The Right Breed For The Job   **37**

Chapter Four: What Makes A Guide Dog   **53**

Chapter Five: The Blue Peter Connection   **62**

PART II: BREEDING, REARING AND TRAINING   **72**

Chapter Six: The Mating Game   **73**

Chapter Seven: Artificial Insemination   **92**

Chapter Eight: Pregnancy And Whelping   **99**

Chapter Nine: The Nursing Bitch And Her Puppies   **108**

Chapter Ten: The Campaign For Early Inoculation   **121**

Chapter Eleven: Questions And Answers On Training   **134**

PART III: HEALTH AND CARE   **147**

Chapter Twelve: The Case For Neutering   **148**

Chapter Thirteen: Health And Nutrition   **151**

Chapter Fourteen: Identifying Ailments   **157**

FOREWORD

THE MAN HIMSELF

Every calling has its professionals, those who give lifelong study where others only scratch the surface. Dog training is a calling: police dogs for law enforcement, rescue dogs, farmers' dogs, dogs in sport, dogs to aid the disabled – all demand insight into the canine mind and body to a degree which cannot be attained by part-timers. If the full-time experts in all these dog-disciplines were asked to nominate an all-round supremo among them – the professionals' professional, so to speak – Derek Freeman, of Guide Dogs for the Blind, would be the choice of most.

It is an honour for me – an amateur, though dedicated – to write this prologue to the self-told life story of a man who has made an unparalleled contribution to our knowledge of dogs, and immensely expanded their potentiality for human service. His achievement is due partly to the quality of the man himself, partly to the opportunity which he has had. As head of the Guide Dogs' Breeding Centre at Bishop's Tachbrook, Warwickshire, and of their puppy-walking service, it has been Derek Freeman's duty to match the characters of the dogs he has sent forward for training to the tasks which they are destined to fulfil. He has therefore been intimately concerned with their subsequent progress through their months of qualification, and he has monitored their years on the busy, traffic-laden streets of modern Britain, each of them with a human life in their care, to be safely delivered at destination after destination, every day of their working lives. When it comes to monitoring, Derek Freeman is in a class by himself. The message of his facts and figures is priceless.

How he has done this is for him to tell, not me. My part is limited to introducing the man himself, though 'limited' may be a misleading word. He himself would disclaim any other accolade than that of a job well done; but because he has so enormously enriched other people in ways more important than money, he deserves recognition for what he is – a great man. I know that I do not exaggerate, having seen him in action during the years in which I served on the General Council of Guide Dogs for the Blind, and in particular on the committee most responsible for the welfare and efficiency of the dogs and their trainers.

What began on Merseyside sixty years ago as a pioneering effort on the borderline of fantasy has become a worldwide success. Though my purpose is to portray Derek Freeman, not the Guide Dog movement, its development here serves as a measure of his stature.

Four thousand Guide Dogs now operate in Britain. Their number continues to increase. Each has to be replaced every seven years on average. All are purpose-bred to be nothing else than Guide Dogs, and only the cream of them are entrusted with a human life. To maintain the canine pool from which they come, and which must be large enough to accommodate the very exacting failure rate, 800 chosen puppies are being 'walked' at any one time, singly in the homes of specially knowledgeable dog owners. Two hundred proven brood bitches, each mated every second season, are providing the intake from which future Guide Dogs are chosen. Simultaneously Britain's seven training centres are teaching 650 grown-up puppies, their 'walk' completed, the techniques of safe conveyance of a sightless human companion along and across our ever-busy streets.

The infrastructure on which this demanding programme is based had Derek Freeman at its heart and head for quarter of a century. It is difficult to think of any instance in which one man has seen more dogs and, while regarding them all with insight and love, has been as clear-headedly critical of them individually. He has had to be, in the interests of those whose lives are destined to depend on them.

In all forms of stockmanship, the man who deals with the greatest number of animals eventually gathers most wisdom. Through the opportunity which life brought him, Derek Freeman has done that. And more. For he has preserved and shared that wisdom. The meticulous records of every stage in the life and training of each individual dog and bitch in the mounting thousands which have entered or failed to enter the Guide Dog service are permanent records of ancestry, management, success and failure. They, and the conclusions to be drawn from them, are an unequalled distillation of practical experience which will be of immense value to future breeders of dogs of all kinds.

Such is this man's life. He can be proud of it as, in a quiet way, he is. And the rest of the world will be for ever grateful. What of the man himself?

Derek Freeman is a Yorkshireman from the clean and Spartan dales where growing lads learn the facts of life the hard way, but are not depressed thereby. It is no surprise that his first dog was a fox terrier, for there is something of a terrier in him still: a merry fun as well as the serious purpose; eyes that flash a varminty look when he meets a kindred spirit. It is unlikely that the young Derek Freeman invariably saw eye to eye with every gamekeeper in his neighbourhood, for in youth his was a free soul. He still loves the countryside with a deep, deep love – as alert as ever to all its possibilities, and the wonders in it.

It was, nevertheless, to the town that he went, and to a career in engineering. Guide dogs and blind people were not the losers thereby. The unbending disciplines under which engineers work and think, gave him the clarity of mind that distinguishes certitude from doubt, and has made his contribution all of a piece, whether it was to Guide Dogs and other dogs, to blind people and other people, or most of all to his family and numberless friends. When Derek Freeman had done a job, nothing rattled. Over now, to him.

Wilson Stephens
April 1991

INTRODUCTION

Breeding, rearing, selecting and training dogs has been my life for forty years. It has brought me many friends and much pleasure, and it has given me and my family the opportunity to travel to France, Germany, Holland, Ireland, Canada, Japan and America, in order to visit Guide Dog schools. In some cases I have been able to assist others engaged in similar work, but in all instances, I acquired new knowledge and made new friends. The Guide Dogs for the Blind Association in Britain has supplied breeding stock, or puppies, to seventeen guide dog schools across the world, and in 1988 The Guide Dogs for the Blind Association hosted a conference attended by the many nations which look to the UK for help in improving their canine stock.

There have been many memorable moments in a career that has seen the GDBA grow to become a world-leader in its field, but there is one highlight that seems to sum up all that has been achieved – the GDBA Golden Jubilee in July 1981, when six hundred guide dogs and their visually-handicapped owners gathered in Westminster Abbey for a Thanksgiving Service. The faultless behaviour of the dogs was the finest possible testimony to the care and dedication of brood and stud holders, puppy walkers, kennel staff, trainers and guide dog owners. The sight of so many valued, well-kept dogs and bitches lying quietly at their masters' or

Derek Freeman pictured with brood bitch 'Seiko' and stud dog 'Peter'.

mistresses' feet during the service, and then the procession of dogs and owners down Birdcage Walk to the Royal Mews, showed all that we had achieved in our breeding, rearing and training programmes. It was said afterwards that only two animals uttered a bark during the hour-and-a-half-long service in the Abbey. The first was a single deep bark, obviously a Labrador male. The second was three sharp barks of a much higher pitch. I said: "That must have been a bitch," and when I was asked how I knew, I replied: "A female never answers back in words of one syllable!"

The main purpose of writing this book is to show the effect that planned breeding, early conditioning and humanization has on rearing a responsive puppy with a pleasant disposition. I have had experience of many adult dogs who lacked this early education, and I have seen the disastrous effect this has had, leaving me in no doubt as to the value of early education for a young puppy. Many of today's problem-dogs have been reared by problem-owners, who are ignorant of the way animals learn. They have failed to understand that the dog is a pack animal. It looks upon its owner and the family as fellow members of the pack. However, if the dog grows up with more determination and self-will than its owners, it will not be long before the dog or bitch elevates itself to pack leader.

If a dog is given proper education and control during rearing, this sets the right pattern. A fair but firm owner, who is totally consistent in what he expects from the dog, rewarding good behaviour at the correct time, will never have a problem dog. The saying "Dogs, like children, mirror their owners," is entirely true, providing the owner has achieved this level of control at the critical stages of a puppy's development, i.e. the early weeks and months of its life. I have seen the benefits of early education and socialization in thousands of puppies in the past twenty-five years, and in all my experience I have found that these turned out to be the more tractable and amenable animals, having a distinct advantage over those that had had a poor start in life.

I consider myself fortunate that I got paid and pensioned for practising what was initially a hobby, starting with the Smooth-haired Terrier I owned when I was nine years old. My interest in dogs took me down several pathways – from poaching, competing in obedience tests and working trials, to breeding, and eventually to a full-time career with The Guide Dogs for the Blind Association. Following my retirement I have worked as a consultant on breeding and puppy rearing for the Association, and I have become a member of the Association of Pet Behaviour Councillors and reguarly help owners to deal with problem pets, who have failed to respond to all proven methods of training. Time and time again, I have found that this is because the owner does not understand his dog and the way the dog perceives things. Some of the experience I have gained has come through swimming against the tide, and making controversial decisions. This happened when I took on veterinary surgeons the length and breadth of the country and proposed the six-week inoculation of puppies. This gives the pups the chance to acquire that early education and socialization, which I believe is so vital to the development of the adult dog. Despite facing such widespread criticism, the early inoculation programme became GDBA policy, and results show how much it has benefited both dog and owner.

Part I

Guide Dogs
For The Blind

Chapter One

LOOKING BACK

When I joined The Guide Dogs for the Blind Association in 1959, it had been training guide dogs for nearly thirty years. The first four dogs (all German Shepherds, or Alsatians, as they were then called) and their blind owners were trained in 1931, and four more qualified the following year. After that, numbers increased very slowly. There were enormous problems of finance, and suitable dogs and training staff were in short supply. However, two training centres, one at Leamington Spa and the other at Exeter, became operational.

Today, seven centres train about 650 dogs and their blind owners every year, and there are nearly 4,000 working guide dogs in Britain. When I started at the Leamington centre, production in the previous twelve months had been 120 'units', and the guide dog population was about 600. Nearly three decades had passed since the first guide dogs were trained in Britain, but dog-supply was still a major problem. They came from a variety of sources, with two dealers, one in Scotland and the other in Wales, supplying the majority. The dogs were sent by rail, with just a label on their collar giving a name. If they came from Scotland they would invariably be called 'Roy', 'Floss', 'Lassie,' or 'Laddie', and on one occasion the kennels at Leamington held eighteen dogs named Roy! The majority of the dogs were males, which presented problems because very few males could be kennelled together, without the risk of an almighty punch-up. The dogs were accepted for a testing period, and if they were then kept the Association paid the dealer £5 plus the carriage. If they were rejected, the dealer would sometimes ask for the dog to be returned, but invariably the dogs were sold for a couple of pounds or so. Only a very small percentage of these dogs qualified as guides; this was because most of them had been brought up on the hills, and they were terribly suspicious of the urban environment. The majority were Border Collies, and were often sound-shy, which is a common breed characteristic. A former member of the training staff, Arthur Phillipson, who later became Director of Training, remembers one little Collie called Roy, who was suspicious of everything. In those days, the dogs were walked from the training centre at Leamington towards the town centre, which was about a mile away. The first part of the walk was in a relatively quiet area, and gradually dog and trainer would progress further and further into the town, until one day, they would walk right into the centre. When Arthur and Roy got to the town centre, a lady came out of a furniture shop and banged the door. Poor Roy panicked. He was standing alongside a bus queue and he disappeared right up a lady's skirt to hide!

A number of dogs were offered to the Association from domestic situations. The owners were asked to fill in a questionnaire about the dog before it was accepted – but we soon found that these were rarely truthful. The new recruits usually travelled by rail, and the Association would send the owner a lead, muzzle and chain, and then a member of staff would collect the dog from Leamington Station. In those days there was only one vehicle available, and so this often meant a long walk into town. Occasionally the dog would be delivered to a small station, which was much closer, and dogs that arrived around 10pm would often be delivered direct to the training centre by a porter. If a dog arrived in the small hours, it would be kept overnight and someone from the centre would collect it the next morning. The worst cases were when dogs arrived at the station unsolicited by the Association. All the paperwork they had was a label attached to their collars, addressed to 'Guide Dogs, Leamington', and we had absolutely no idea where they had come from. Obviously, this meant we had no way of returning the dog, which was, no doubt, what the sender intended.

Quite a few of the dogs came from the London area, or travelled through London, and they would be chained up in the guard's van. Many of them arrived on the late night train, which was in fact a through-train stopping at Leamington Station for about a minute. There was therefore little time to get into the train and get the dog unhooked, particularly if it was rather aggressive. Many of the dogs had chewed through the muzzles sent by the Association, and frequently the dog had not been muzzled in the first place. It was suggested that the best way to unhook an aggressive dog was to get behind it, and then hustle it out of the van. Trainers were advised to get on a lower level than the dog, so they would get on their belly and wriggle up slowly, often with the animal snarling and growling. Often all attempts failed, and there were occasions when the guard's van had to be unhitched, and the train went on without it.

Dogs offered by the public still arrived by rail well into the sixties, even though our own Puppy Walking Scheme was established by then. I remember arriving back after a day attempting to track down suitable puppies, and there was an urgent message asking us to go down to Leamington Station to collect a bitch. It was a German Shepherd, and they were having difficulty in getting her off the train. When I arrived, the train was still standing in the station but was due to go on to Birmingham and the train driver was insisting on pulling out. I flew up the steps, and on my way I spotted a member of British rail staff having his hand dressed – a victim of the German Shepherd. I got to the guard's van to find three or four station employees standing by the sliding door and peeping in. The bitch was going absolutely berserk at the end of her chain. One of the station employees said: "Be careful, she has just bitten one of our staff who tried to get her off the train with a piece of sacking". If you want to torment a dog, wave a piece of sacking at it. Any dog that has got some aggression in it, or is inclined to bite, will have a go at the sacking, and this, of course, is what had happened. It appeared as though they all wanted to see me as the next victim, and I was surrounded by a rapt audience as I stepped into the van. In fact, their presence only served to aggravate the poor bitch. I quickly turned round on them, asked them to go away, and shut the door behind them. I spent the next five minutes edging cautiously up to the back of the van. The bitch was on a chain and the muzzle was, unfortunately, tied to a rail behind her. This seemed to be a plan cunningly devised by the railway staff to make the job as difficult as possible. Eventually, after a lot of threats and a lot of snapping and flashing of teeth, I managed to get hold of the chain that was securely tied around the rail. As I got hold if it, I reassured the bitch, and I was just beginning to build up a rapport with her when, suddenly, the van door was flung open. I was just standing up, and the bitch caught me on the elbow, tearing through my jacket and shirt to the skin. She had been startled, and she thought she was going to be cornered. Eventually, I won her confidence sufficiently to get her out of the van, and the train pulled away. I don't know what explanation was given out over the tannoy at Birmingham New Street for its late arrival!

The next problem was to get the bitch into my van, and on the way out of the station I suddenly remembered that I already had two dogs in it – a German

Shepherd and a Standard Poodle. Unfortunately, the Poodle had managed to get through the cage in the back and was sitting contentedly on the front seat. The German Shepherd was my own bitch, and she was still sitting obediently in the back, wagging her tail as I approached. I enlisted the help of a sympathetic station employee, who courageously said he would open the back of the van for me. However, he soon changed his mind when he saw my bitch sitting there: he had just seen what a German Shepherd could do! "No way mate, you're on your own," he said. I was therefore faced with trying to bundle a very frightened and aggressive animal in with my highly exuberant bitch, who was waiting to bounce all over us. Fortunately, my bitch jumped out, and, out of pure fright, the newcomer leapt straight into the van.

Experiences like this were not uncommon, but I am glad to say that protective aggression is very rare in the Association's present-day stock. It would be wrong not to highlight the encounter. One staff member, Marion Shipley, who eventually became a Puppy Walking Supervisor, recalls picking up a large male Collie, named Spring, from the station at around breakfast time. Spring had come from a remote Scottish island, and so he was not used to busy urban areas. However, he showed no fear of anything he met on the walk back to the centre. He was very friendly, adapted well to the kennel routine, and settled easily into training. Unfortunately, he succumbed to distemper and had to be put to sleep. Disease was a severe problem. The dogs didn't suffer from 'hard pad', but there was the common distemper, and the dogs needed to be vaccinated. A live vaccine was used, and this could present real problems. The dogs came from so many places that the disease was frequently introduced to the centre, and we had to isolate it, as best we could. The effect of an infectious disease on kennels can be devastating, and when para distemper first hit the country, eighteen of the dogs, housed in the two kennel blocks, had to be put to sleep. The local vet spent the whole of Christmas Day at the centre, and the staff spent the whole time taking the corpses to the destructor in Leamington to be burnt. The poor dogs were dying like flies, and there was nothing that could be done, for, at this stage, no-one knew what the disease was. Burroughs Wellcome quickly developed a serum, which helped, but by that time, almost all the Association's dogs which had been in kennels had been lost. Until the vaccine was developed and used, distemper was a constant headache.

At this stage most of the dogs were not neutered, and this caused another set of problems. Neutering was not an accepted practice, and many people disapproved of it. Certainly, the public were very against it, and as the Association relied so much on the public for support, it did not want to do anything that might offend them. Naturally, a bitch in season unsettled all the males in kennels. In training, Amplex tablets or Amplex Wash was used to try and mask the scent. Needless to say, this was not a very satisfactory procedure.

The Association were offered plenty of dogs that people did not want, but sometimes the reverse situation happened. Leamington police found a little Collie-cross, which they handed to us. She took to her training very well and one Saturday morning Arthur Phillipson was working with the dog in the town centre when a half-drunken man came up to him and said: "Hey, that's my dog!" Arthur pointed out that the bitch had come from the police, and a lot of time and effort had been spent on her training. However, when the man called the bitch by her proper name, she wagged her tail and got very excited. Clearly, the man was right. Later it was discovered the bitch was nine years old, which illustrates another problem that was faced in those days: the Association often had no idea how old the dogs were. The dealers knew we didn't want animals over two years old, and it was strange that no matter what dog they sent us, it never seemed to be over the age of two!

The majority of dogs were rejected at that time because of sound-shyness. Many were not conditioned to town-life, and some dogs became extremely suspicious if they were kept in close contact with humans. They were quite happy on a long leash, but when they were put in a harness they got into a terrible panic at their area of independence being restricted. Collies were always very sensitive to their surroundings, and they only suited a limited number of blind people: those with very good balance, who were light on their feet. The so-called 'left tendency' was also a problem. As the name implies, the dog pulls strongly to the left, and this happens particularly if handlers are a bit unsteady on their feet. This tendency would result in dogs scraping against walls, and it was not unknown for them to wear away their harness on the left-hand side.

In the early fifties, the Association had a very few German Shepherds and very few gun dogs. The Director of Training, Captain Liakhoff, did not like Labrador Retrievers because he believed that they were inclined to get too fat. He was very keen on German Shepherds, but there were very few to choose from because so many people had given them as war dogs, and those that were left were not always of the highest quality. However, the breed was popular with the public, and there were those who were quick to cash in on the shortage of dogs. As a result, a lot of indiscriminate breeding went on, and it took some years before temperament was stabilised. Many of the German Shepherds handled by the Association at this time were very nervy and aggressive.

It is worth recalling that working conditions for blind people and their dogs were very different in the late forties and fifties. If you waited until 9am when everybody had gone to work, you could stand in the middle of the main road outside

Leamington Training Centre and direct any form of training, without fear of being mown down. Now you are fortunate if you can drive out of the gate without waiting for twenty minutes. The dogs that were used in the early fifties, or before, would not have been able to stand up to present conditions. They would have been totally unsuitable. Today, a dog must be conditioned from a very early age to the hectic environment in which it will have to work.

In 1950 a second Training Centre was opened at Exeter. Demand for guide dogs was increasing, and the waiting list for a blind applicant was about five years, compared with six months at present. The supply of dogs remained erratic, and the quality was generally poor. It was becoming increasingly clear that a properly organised scheme for rearing puppies was needed to improve the situation. The value of puppy walking had been recognised for many years, but attempts to introduce schemes had never got very far.

Eventually, Arthur Phillipson went to America to visit the guide dog schools there. He investigated two puppy walking schemes, one run by The Seeing Eye, the other by Guide Dogs for the Blind, in California. Arthur was particularly impressed with the Californian scheme, which operated through the Four H Youth Schemes. However, it lacked professional supervision and many puppies were placed at great distances from the centre. Callum McLean, who was a member of the Association's General Council, had read about the Four H Puppy Walking Scheme, and he was convinced that something similar was needed in Britain. He started a small experimental scheme in the Chobham area in Surrey, and he gradually built it up. Arthur would go down to help, sometimes acquiring puppies, which he would then assist in supervising. Another pilot scheme was tested in the North London area. One of the puppy walkers was the wife of a taxi driver who was so fed-up with her husband's working hours that she started rearing a puppy. She made a good job of it, and when her husband told his colleagues about it, the families of three other London taxi drivers reared pups for the Association in the Barnet area.

The scheme, although still small, was beginning to prove itself, and it was obvious that if it was going to grow someone had to be taken on to organise it on a larger scale. An advertisement was placed in *Dog World* asking for someone interested in German Shepherd Dogs, who would be required to develop a Puppy Walking Scheme rapidly. The qualifications were stated as a knowledge of the training and rearing of dogs, but most of all, a person who was prepared to work hard. *Dog World* was one of the two dog papers that we got every Friday, and I would read nearly every word in both. My wife, Margaret, actually spotted the ad before me and said: "Here's just the job you're after." We were living in Yorkshire and were both active members of various local canine societies, as well as three dog training clubs – the

British Alsatian Association (Leeds Branch), West Yorkshire Alsatian Training Club (Bradford) and ASPADS 1st Yorkshire Branch (Otley). I wanted to leave the engineering firm, where I was employed, in order to work with dogs, and I had applied for a number of jobs. I had already been on the short-list for the Royal Airforce as Chief Civilian Instructor. I had also toyed with the idea of becoming a gamekeeper, but I had lost interest when I was told I would be expected to walk her ladyship's dogs every morning at five o'clock, light the fires in the mansion, chop the logs and hump the coal in!

About ten days after sending off my application for the job with guide dogs I was asked to go down for an interview in London. I had never been as far afield as London, and it was a great occasion for me. I can remember racing down to Otley Station on my motorcycle and leaving it parked, unlocked, outside against a wall – a thing you couldn't do nowadays. In London I caught the tube to Green Park Station, and I went to the head office in Piccadilly, only a couple of doors away from the Kennel Club. I was interviewed by Arthur Phillipson for about half an hour and we were then joined by Charles Maton, who was the General Manager of the Association. I was grilled about my interest in dogs, and the extent of my knowledge of different breeds. I was asked whether I held a driving licence. In fact, I had a motorcycle licence and had just passed my driving test in a car – a 1928 Austin. Little did I realise that I would soon be driving all over the country, searching for stock for training, and would be supervising the Puppy Walking Scheme. I was asked by Mr Phillipson if I had dogs of my own, and when I replied that I had four, I was told that if I was offered the job I would be required to live on-site, and I would not be able to bring my dogs with me. The plan was to build a new reception kennel, away from the main Training Centre at Leamington, and I would be expected to live on the premises.

I left the interview knowing that there were other people to be seen, and I thought "Well, that's the end of that." I really didn't know whether I had made an impression or not, but I was sure that I did not want to give up my four dogs. I had made that known in the broadest of Yorkshire dialect, and I was certain that would ruin my chances. A week went by, and I got a letter saying that the job was mine, subject to a second interview. I spent a day at Leamington, and managed to convince the management that I was the right man for the job. I was offered £11.10 shillings a week plus accommodation, which I accepted, even though I was earning £22 a week back in Yorkshire. However, to put things in perspective, Arthur Phillipson, who was Director of Training, was only earning £17 a week, and had started in the early fifties on £2 a week. So I accepted and was asked to start on 12 January 1959 as reception kennel manager. I was very concerned at having to leave my wife,

Margaret, and our dogs behind for a six-month probationary period. If I wasn't going to be suited to the job, there would be no point in my wife moving. However, by the October I had begun to settle down, although I still felt a little out of place at mealtimes around the large dining-room table. I was generally flanked by trainers who were much younger than myself, and at the top was a retired Royal Air Force officer, who was the administrator. He generally kept the peace, and he was readily available as a referee to sort out disputes and offer advice. Most of the staff came from south of Watford; coming from the dales of Yorkshire, I was very conscious of my broad accent. For a long time I was loath to join in conversations. I simply answered questions, which must seem very strange to those who know how much I like to talk. Eventually I accepted that these young men could not have cared less about my accent. They were very friendly and helped me settle in and understand the job. There was never a time when I could not get help or advice, or receive a warm welcome when I returned to the centre after a long and fruitless journey trying to find suitable dogs for training.

The Association keeps a monthly register of dogs, and the entry for November 1959 sums up the situation we were facing. It shows that twenty-two dogs entered kennels for testing, and only three turned out to be of any value. One was called Reiner, later to become the first German Shepherd brood bitch. The other two became guide dogs, one staying to be trained at Leamington Spa, the other going down to Exeter. The remainder were of no use to the Association. Two were returned to their previous owners, one died of distemper and the others were sold. One of the recruits was found to be in whelp. She was a Curly Coated Retriever, and I was shocked to see that, due to lack of space and proper facilities, the resulting litter was put down by the local vet. This naturally caused the bitch to go into shock, and she had to be sedated. She was distressed for some time, and eventually she lost all her coat and became quite distressed. This incident made me determined that once I had more authority, nothing like it would ever happen again. It also highlighted the need to fight for better facilities. During that eventful month five puppies also arrived at the centre – donated, bearing no name or address. They were very poor quality specimens, worm-ridden, and generally unhealthy – quite unsuitable for placing with any puppy walker.

It is interesting to note that the breeds of dog recorded in the register included German Shepherds, Golden Retrievers, Boxers, Collies and Labradors. However, there were not many Labradors, as purchase prices ranged from 30 shillings to the magnificent sum of nine guineas. The prices obtained by selling them if they were rejected was small, usually between £1 and seven guineas, despite the fact that they had been cared for and that they were in better condition after several weeks of

Early recruits: 'Peggy' : Rough Collie.   *'Shadow' : Alaskan Malamute.*

'Juno' : Labrador x Newfoundland.   *'Topps' : Boxer.*

feeding, housing and veterinary care.

The catchment area for incoming dogs was vast, extending the length and breadth of Britain. Many of the dogs had never travelled before, and had never lived in kennels, so it was a traumatic experience for sensitive animals to be suddenly subjected to this new, noisy environment, even if it was clean, and there was bedding to sleep on. The kennels were constructed of pressed concrete slabs with an asbestos roof and they were badly insulated, making them cold in winter and hot in summer. The windows were small with frosted glass, and were far too high for the dogs to see out of. The same applied to the doors, which were solid wood covered in a galvanised steel sheet on the inside, with a peephole at about four foot high for staff to view the animals. I think it would be fair to say that the kennels were reminiscent of a maximum security prison. Many doors were, in fact, stripped of their galvanised cladding by distraught inmates during the night. The yards and runs were pack-runs, and although they were of extremely generous dimensions, they had a tarmacadam surface, which made them time-consuming to clean. The brick or concrete walls surrounding the dog runs at Leamington were a minimum of six feet six inches high, and they gave staff no chance to observe the dogs, or vice versa. In fact, many a dog was accidently left out in the run during the winter months, and it was only through the diligence of very caring staff, who lived in at the time, that many were discovered.

The combination of straw bedding, wooden boards, and surface drains also made it virtually impossible to prevent the spread of disease. Thankfully, all that has changed, and today's first-rate kennels allow maximum observation of stock and they are designed to be labour-saving in order to give staff more time to spend with the dogs. However, one must not get things out of proportion. I don't think that the kennels in the fifties shocked me, because most kennels in the country at that time were nothing very special. It was the accepted way to keep dogs, and, generally speaking, the animals were contented. But I had my own ideas about how the kennels should be run: I wanted stock to be able to see each other, I wanted human contact to be established, and I wanted the staff to be able to see the animals most of the time and vice versa.

The first step I took in this direction was to try to persuade the Association to improve the puppy kennel by adding grill-gates and tip-up beds. I also suggested having the walls inside the kennels painted white, and a one-foot-deep bitumastic strip at floor level on the walls to protect them from splashes as we mopped and swilled them. I felt sure that light, well-ventilated kennels, in which the pups could establish contact through grill gates, would be less stressful and would help us to achieve a higher success rate. However, I was told that a charity was not able to spend money on such luxuries, and most dogs would be quite content in a loose box with plenty of straw. Hygiene could be maintained with an annual lime wash. A lot of gundogs were kept that way and lived a perfectly normal life. My argument was that we were looking for something rather special in our dogs, even at that time. I knew that kennel construction would have to change if we were to improve the success-rate of both puppies and adults.

One of my first major projects was to develop the Puppy Walking Scheme and to improve the quality of puppies. We were still heavily reliant on adult stock coming in direct for training. To acquire puppies we had to get to know breeders throughout the country, and it was a long time before I began to discover where the better dogs came from. Fortunately I had some extremely good contacts within the dog fraternity prior to coming to GDBA. I realised after a while that good puppies were available, but we would have to pay a good price for them. What finally convinced me was when one day a woman arrived, without prior warning, at the Training Centre with seven puny little puppies. They were sodden in urine and most had been violently sick. They were, in fact, the remnants of a litter she had not "been able to get rid of" – her words – and she came to us thinking that because we were a charity we would be only too pleased to have them. This attitude was not uncommon at the time. None of the puppies were anything like the calibre I wanted, so I turned them down, much to the breeder's annoyance, for she had travelled a long way to bring the puppies to us. But I felt I could not afford to take the risk. Puppy walkers were scarce, and if a sickly puppy was lost through illness, the puppy walker, who would have become attached to the dog, might well become disillusioned.

About ten days later, and without official blessing, I bought a quality Labrador puppy and promised the breeder £10 for it. It was the first time I had actually paid for a pup. However, I did not realise that the breeder was a friend of the woman who had brought her urine-sodden litter to us ten days previously. She promptly wrote to the General Manager, and I was asked to explain my actions – in no uncertain terms. I pointed out that we required quality puppies if we were to succeed, and finally it was agreed that I should be allowed to purchase a number of puppies at a realistic price. However, it was stressed that we were a charity, and I should therefore attempt to get puppies free of charge. Today we still acquire quality pups by donation, or at a concessionary rate, if we can; but if we cannot and if good puppies are offered, we will pay a good price for them. Nowadays, of course, most of the pups come from our breeding programme, and we take very few from other sources. Our reliance on dealers often led us into difficult situations. One dealer, who had supplied us with adult stock and puppies, had a large kennel area at her home, and she also owned a block of terraced houses, and literally every room was packed with dogs. I remember going there on one occasion and she must have had at least thirty litters – there were dogs in the toilets, pantries, coal stores, outhouses, and in boxes under the sink. She sent dogs all over the world, I believe, and had supplied us with a few adults that had been successful, as well as a few pups. I went to acquire a couple of pups, but I found they were not old enough to bring away. At the time we were placing puppies of between ten and twelve weeks of age on puppy-walking schemes – not six weeks as we do at present. I arranged to return and collect the pups when they were a little older, but she rang me up about a week later and asked if I could get the puppies away quickly because she thought she might have distemper starting in the kennels. I drove over to have a look. She didn't have distemper starting – half the stock had got it, including our two, and it was obviously a very virile virus. One pup had to be put down immediately, the other, a Golden Retriever called Cider, I brought back to the centre. We had to isolate her, as best we could, in a makeshift kennel; we didn't have the marvellous isolation kennels we have now. The pup survived, but was never a robust bitch as an adult. Its second dentition was affected through its contact with distemper, and most of the enamel was missing. However, she trained well, after being successfully puppy walked, and qualified as a working dog.

Events like this really brought home to me the need to start breeding our own stock in large numbers. I therefore began searching for and acquiring suitable brood bitches. At that time we planned to use known and approved stud dogs, but these would be privately owned. The first official brood bitch was a German Shepherd, which was in keeping with the need to bring bigger dogs into training. This particular bitch, Reiner, was offered to us as an adult for training. Her pedigree showed that she was by a post-war champion, a dog called Cito Von Der Meerswatch, who was an early post-war import from Germany. He had been in the country for some time, and where he had been used on good-quality bitches, he had produced a lot of nice puppies. They seemed to have a nice equable temperament, which was what we wanted. Reiner was a top-quality daughter of excellent character by Cito, out of a good Bablake bitch. In order to stamp a good, equable temperament into her puppies, I in-bred her back to her father, who was owned by a breeder called Mrs Beck, of the Letton prefix.

Reiner whelped at my own home because I had now moved out of the training centre. The four puppies were rather puny and weak; possibly in-breeding contributed to this lack of vigour. There were two bitches and two dogs. Sadly, the two bitches succumbed within the first twenty-four hours, despite my wife's efforts to save them, but we were pleased that the two males survived after a lengthy struggle. The two bitches had been born at about eight ounces and the males at ten

'Jock' and 'Mac' : The first dogs purpose-bred by Guide Dogs.

ounces. The two male survivors, Mac and Jock, went on to the puppy-walking scheme, developed into quality dogs of good substance, and eventually qualified as guide dogs. Mac worked for many years in Leamington Spa with a guide dog owner named Mr Moore. Jock also worked for a long time with a Mr McGregor, who lived in Kilpatrick in Scotland.

At this time males were in a minority as guide dogs and were castrated at an early age. We seemed to prefer to train bitches. The change began with the build-up of the puppy-walking scheme and the start of our own serious breeding scheme, from which fifty per cent of the pups could be expected to be males. It seemed terribly wasteful to maintain a bitch, breed puppies and then discard half of them. It therefore became important to try to breed puppies of both sexes with suitable characteristics for training as guide dogs. It was some years later that the biggest step was taken in this direction with cross-bred animals, when we discovered that we could produce males that were just as receptive as bitches to training and work as guide dogs. Now, with either thoroughbred or cross-bred animals, fifty per cent or more of the dogs trained are males.

Chapter Two

BIRTH OF THE BREEDING CENTRE

As the puppy-walking scheme grew during the sixties, the idea of having a separate breeding establishment away from the Leamington training centre gained ground. We needed more space, and I wanted more sterile conditions to help prevent the introduction and spread of disease. We were at that time supplying four Training Centres, Exeter, Leamington Spa, Bolton and Forfar, and consequently the volume of puppies that we were dealing with coming through the Leamington Centre was creating terrible congestion. We were also conscious that the Association was still growing, and the number of guide dogs required was likely to increase. This has indeed proved to be the case, with seven Training Centres now in operation. We had looked at a number of properties, when Tollgate House on the Banbury Road, a few miles from Warwick, came on the market. It was a substantial country house with a garage for five cars, six loose boxes and two large greenhouses situated in nine acres in an ideal situation. We got it for £27,000. Funding for the acquisition of house, land and kennels was through a generous donation from the Charterhouse organisation. The authorities approved our plans for the kennels, but they were not so keen on allowing accommodation to be built for the Breeding Manager. We pointed out that they had allowed accommodation to be built for the manager of the crematorium opposite and that his stock did not take as much looking after as ours, but we had to go to appeal before getting permission to build a bungalow!

Immediately I knew that Tollgate was on the cards, my first priority was to draw up plans in order to get the kennel environment correct. By that time I had already gained quite a lot of knowledge about the layout of kennels, as I had worked in the old badly-designed units at Leamington before the first major rebuilding was carried out. The old kennels had been all separate units located a fair distance from each other. As I sat in my office, I used to observe the waste of staff-time, particularly in the winter, with kennel girls putting dogs out in runs, going back to the food room, and then having to go back to the runs and return the dog to the kennels as soon as the weather changed. This happened, on average, two or three times in a day, every day of the week. I decided that if I was given the opportunity of planning my own kennels, they would be very different to this impractical layout. I wanted a design that would allow complete segregation of dogs, but with all the services coming to one point, all built under one roof, offering shelter and maximum visibility for dogs and staff.

However, the Association at that time still had faith in using professional architects, although, to my mind, these were professional as far as building houses for humans was concerned, but when it came to designing first-class kennels for dogs, they were amateurs. I well remember the first kennel which was purely architect-designed. It was a perimeter kennel with no trap-gates, in which no man on two legs could catch a dog on four, if the dog escaped. It had no place to hang a brush, no sink units, no heating, and no beds. My chance to put forward my own ideas came when I had the opportunity to speak to the Association's Chairman of that time, Sir Joseph Napier. I stressed to him the importance of using expertise from within to build a first-class kennel. We could use our own knowledge and practical experience and profit from not repeating mistakes with kennels and buildings that had previously been designed and built for dogs. We had already built some worthwhile, practical kennels, such as the approval block and whelping block at Leamington Spa, and I said that if the Puppy Walking and Breeding Scheme was to move out of Leamington Spa Training Centre, I would like some assurance that we would not be stepping back to the 1959 era and inheriting a Nissen hut with packing cases as our future home. Sir Joseph replied: "Freeman, if you can provide details of the kennel you require and it is a practical proposition, we will provide the funding to produce that kennel. But you will have to prove your point and present a worthwhile plan." I felt this was a remarkably enlightened response, and it gave me a unique opportunity of putting my ideas into practice. At Leamington, we had largely been modifying and altering the old kennels – now we had the chance to start from scratch.

As soon as I got home after the day's work, I got out my pencils, ruler and an old roll of wallpaper and started sketching. I had already got a broad idea of what I wanted, and I also got the staff interested in the plans, requesting their ideas, and their criticisms of the present design of kennels. It was not long before I was snowed under with ideas, which I found very heartening as it indicated their interest and their depth of awareness for the welfare and care of stock at all levels. The result, after burning a lot of midnight oil, was the present H-block, which stands at Tollgate – the forerunner of all present-day training blocks at the Association's seven Training Centres.

The H-block design was considered revolutionary at the time, but the idea behind it was purely practical. I wanted a layout where stock could have maximum observation, and, at the same time, the staff could see all that was going on. I believed there was a great need to be able to immediately segregate stock, as opposed to isolate stock. For example: the stud dogs needed to be kept in one section of a kennel away from the bitches which would be in a breeding term. The H-block design gave the opportunity for four independent kennel blocks, within the four legs, plus independent kennel units within the cenre which enabled us to segregate six classifications of dogs:

1. WHELPING BLOCK: For whelping bitches and their families from birth to six weeks of age.
2. HOSPITALISATION BLOCK: Mainly used as a recovery block, as operations are not done on the premises.
3. BOARDING BLOCK: For puppies coming in for observation while they are still on the Puppy Scheme. This block is used to condition puppies to kennel environment, which is invaluable with certain breeds, and for the more sensitive dogs and bitches.
4. ASSESSMENT BLOCK: These are puppies returning after their full term of puppy walking and coming in for assessment prior to going through to training or selection as breeding animals. Those assessed go on to one of the seven Training Centres. Again, with segregation, you can work to routines, bringing dogs in at the beginning of the month and grouping them, and then sending them off at the end of the month.

5. BROOD BITCH BLOCK: To house the many brood bitches that were in breeding term, coming in for mating or for security reasons. Security, in this case refered to ensuring that bitches in season that were not being used for breeding, did not get misaligned while out in a home or in kennels (nowadays all our 200 brood bitches are linked with Brood Bitch Holders, and live in homes).

6. STUD DOG BLOCK: In the opposite leg we house male studs, many of which are resident on the premises, and a number of which are regularly alternated with studs that are housed with Stud Dog Owners.

In the H-block layout there is a centre main-entry corridor which can be cleaned by disinfecting daily, and all the ancillary rooms such as the dog kitchen, walk-in fridge, kennel manager's office, dispensary and food room are adjacent to it. Also integral in the block are toilets, with hand-washing facilities, bedding room for storage of the shredded paper or wood-wool, a weighing room, and a boiler room to facilitate the heating of the total complex. I envisaged that the volume of stock we were handling would increase, with the growing demand for guide dogs. The H Block was therefore designed so that it could be extended easily to take us into the 21st century, and could cope with a maximum of 200 dogs at any one time – yet still giving maximum comfort and security to all inmates.

As well as the H-block, it was imperative that we had three other independent units. The most important of these was an isolation unit for sick animals, suffering from infectious or contagious diseases, which under no circumstances could be placed in the main H-block. We were going to have hundreds of young uninoculated stock on the premises, a large moving population of dogs, and also extremely valuable breeding animals, including brood bitches which could be particularly vulnerable while they were whelping and nursing litters. When we designed the isolation block, the worst type of health hazards we were dealing with were distemper, mange, and kennel cough, but subsequently we were confronted with a much more difficult disease in the form of Parvovirus. Without the isolation facilities, the impact of this disease on a Breeding Centre could have been disastrous. In fact, we only lost lost six puppies at the period when Parvovirus was at its height. There are many views about the validity of kennels having total isolation, because of the cost-effectiveness. Personally, I would prefer our isolation block to be empty for 365 days in the year, which would indicate that we had no problems. Equally, if the unit is empty for 364 days and we get a Parvo case on the 365th day, then you have a facility to isolate and protect the other valuable stock from this dreaded virus. If we had not built an isolation unit, it could have cost the Association thousands of pounds in valuable training and breeding dogs, many of which could not be replaced, quite apart from the distress caused to animals and the anxiety that would be placed on staff, puppy walkers and brood bitch owners, that have to care for these dogs under difficult circumstances.

I had to wait quite a time before we could go ahead with my next project – a mating room and small dispensary for processing Artificial Insemination, which would accommodate the instruments and microscopes and equipment for checking sperm counts and vaginal smears from the bitches. The mating room is basically a room with a non-slippery, easy-to-clean floor surface, slightly graded, enabling us to swill out the floors and walls quite easily to ensure maximum hygiene. Bitches and dogs can mate in comparative ease and can relax and have room to move in play; thus they are able to stimulate one another in a conducive atmosphere without interference.

Another individual unit, which has already paid dividends, is the Intake Block for puppies in transit. This is a six-kennel block complete with its own food room, food store and utility washing area, which houses young puppies coming in from brood bitch owners at six weeks of age, when the litters are split up. Ideally, they come into the Puppy Holding Unit for a maximum period of three days prior to being transported to one of the seven Training Centres. Rather than subject them to long journeys immediately the litter is broken up, they are brought to this block, where they are cossetted, fed and housed, checked over and evaluated. Then they are collected by the Puppy Supervisors and are transported to their individual puppy walker, after having their first inoculations against Hardpad, Distemper, Hepatitis Leptospirosis and Parvovirus. Potentially, this could be a stressful situation for a young litter, but the very fact that they come collectively as a litter into the block, and are cared for by a sympathetic, qualified, professional kennel staff member, does much to avoid this. The majority of the puppies are soon playing vigorously with one another and eating heartily when their first meal is presented.

At the Breeding Centre we also needed generous grass paddocks for recreation and relief for resident dogs on site (except isolation dogs). The main grass paddocks are located away from the main blocks but still within reach of the kennel staff so that they can see and hear what is going on, to enable them to control the dogs at exercise. The isolation block, hospital and whelping blocks have their own individual relief runs. All runs for hospitalised dogs and whelping bitches are fully covered for maximum protection. Surrounding the H-block on the extremities, right up to the walls of the individual kennels, are concrete runs for dogs to use for immediate relief. Wire-mesh, easy-to-remove panels come down to ground level to afford maximum observation for stock and staff alike. I remember arguing for runs of that design at the Leamington Training Centre, while the opposition wanted to retain runs with high brick walls, saying that wire-mesh runs would only aggravate dogs making noise because they would constantly be stirred up by seeing so many different distractions. My answer was that if dogs were managed correctly, in proper accommodation which stimulated them and kept them happy, then there was no earthly reason why we should have a noisy kennel, particularly when dogs were handled by professionally trained staff. Thankfully, I won the battle, and after keeping literally thousands of dogs in runs with good visibility for over twenty years, I know that the value to dogs and staff is immeasurable.

Inevitably, there was a lot of hard work and heartache before we were ready to move into Tollgate House, and in November 1969 the Breeding and Puppy Walking Centre was officially opened by Princess Alexandra, patron of the Association. The centre became fully operational in May 1970. We started with a staff of four kennel girls, but despite the fact that our kennels are deliberately labour-saving, we soon had to increase the number of staff, and this trend has continued progressively as the volume of stock has grown. I am sure that people who run commercial kennels would be amazed at the number of staff members per dog. There are many factors involved in this. Firstly, it is important to remember that staff do require adequate time off and so additional cover is always needed, and secondly, I believe that education is paramount, and time must be allowed in the normal working day for this. There is no doubt that the staffing ratio is to the dogs' advantage.

Although some work has taken place since the original building – we now have tiled kennels and corridors throughout – the basic concept remains unaltered. The buildings themselves are of brick construction, with flat insulated roofs over the four legs of the H and a flat roof over the central work area of the H, with pitched roofs spanning each pair of legs, North and South, and covering internal runs between the legs of each pair. The outside runs have partial semi-transparent coverage, so the dogs can shelter if necessary or get into shade. The runs themselves have strong square wire mesh with access via a gate to the outside and to the kennel via french windows. The mesh is six foot high enabling the dogs can see each other. The run surface itself is concrete with a concrete upstand of about six inches between each run to stop the cross-flow of surface water and excreta. Each run is approximately twenty foot long with a generous slope away from the kennel area down to a central drainage system which runs outside each run. Each of these runs can accommodate up to eight dogs in comfort, and I should stress that I feel that it is not only desirable, but essential, that dogs can be mixed in packs and that observation can be undertaken when carrying this out so that they develop an amicable relationship with each other. It is rare for an individual dog to be isolated in a run, except when it is enjoying a raw bone, mutton or a sheep's head. Each run has its own water tap for

One of Tollgate's purpose-built kennels in the stud block.

The concrete runs give partial shelter, and the strong wire-mesh fence allows maximum visibility for dogs and staff.

drinking water, and this makes it easy for the staff to obtain fresh water for the water buckets, and they can use the same water-source for hosing down. Each tap is placed approximately four foot off the ground and has pipework fed from the inside of the block to prevent freezing up. Each kennel which leads off these runs has a french window, strengthened with Georgian wired glass to prevent serious injury to dogs should they bash against them in their exuberance, but allowing maximum vision. The door is mounted so that it is about eight inches above the level of the kennel floor, thus preventing ground draught. Each kennel can house up to four dogs, so that two kennels can be run together when exercising in the adjoining run. There is a raised bed, which is protected around the perimeter with aluminium, and it is made of marine bonded ply covered in white formica. This is mounted on a roll bar and supported by half-bearings, which allows the kennel staff to tip the bed to clean underneath, and drain and subsequently dry it, while it is retained in the vertical position. Generally speaking, our dogs do not require any other form of bedding and do not suffer from any kennel sores or discomfort. If, however, it is felt necessary to cosset an older inmate, then we use sterile paper in a tray, or, put a blanket down.

The kennel floor is graded to allow any water to run off and there is a metal bar gate from the kennel out to a corridor, which runs the entire length of each block. Sunk in the floor is a glazed groove running the entire length of the block for drainage both from the corridor and the kennels. This design also allows staff to let out an individual dog direct from the kennel into the run without running the gauntlet of the entire pack, and in inclement weather they can bring dogs in from the runs and clean them up without making the entire block filthy. I know that a lot of our modern kennels at the newer Training Centres have acoustic cladding in the roof areas to help minimise the noise because of their close proximity to local houses. This has never been a problem at Tollgate because of its rural setting, but I also believe that kennel staff have a responsibility for keeping the noise down by educating and controlling dogs, thus reducing the chance of fighting through excitability.

Each leg of the kennel originally had ten kennels which could house a maximum of forty dogs. We have recently extended two legs for studs and broods. The three inner kennel walls of the kennel units have gaps at the top – they are not joined to the ceiling. This was because I thought that if we ever needed to fumigate completely, then this would afford the ideal way of doing it, and this facility has been used to good advantage on numerous occasions. If you cross over the corridor from a kennel there are observation windows which look into the internal runs, which are between two legs of the H. This obviously gives maximum observation of all stock that are in runs at the time, and I insisted on having an emergency door leading into these internal runs halfway down the corridor, should the need arise for a member of staff to get through there quickly. Finally, each block has a utility area at the end for preparing food and for cleaning all utensils and for waste disposal, sluice and storage of cleaning materials. There is also a sink unit sunk into the floor for hanging the brushes and for cleaning them, in order to keep them as sterile as possible. There is also a grooming table and tackle box with a drop-leaf table provided in each block.

Obviously, we put a lot of thought into the design of the Whelping Block. The whelping kennels are seven foot by four foot, with a low bed that can be tipped up, each having a raised upstand to the front to retain bedding and to stop the young stock from falling out. This in fact can also be tipped down at an angle to the floor, which creates a ramp when the puppies are at that stage when they can cope with it, which is approximately four weeks of age. Each kennel has a sanctuary, and the bitch is taught to get up on to this so that she can rest and observe her stock from a vantage point, without being harassed. The expectant Mum and her litter are not expected to lie directly on the formica; bedding is provided in the form of shredded sterile paper, which has good thermal qualities and is easily cleaned and stored. It is also economical, and unlike straw it does not degenerate to dust and it does not harbour mites. Above each bed there is a heat lamp which is set on a chain at such a height that it cannot over-heat and thus dehydrate the bitch. This is used as required and is thermostatically controlled, set at 70F. In fact, the entire kennel block is centrally heated, but in the event of a failure of the boiler, these heat lamps which are electrically operated will come on, so there is no risk of a bitch and her puppies being chilled.

There is a dispensary containing all the treatments which may be needed in a hurry. A later addition was a shower unit with which you can swill the bitch off and clean her up and make her feel more comfortable after whelping. This particular kennel block is segregated from the main house, and, because the Breeding Centre is located in a rural, isolated spot, we installed television monitor cameras which are wired to a monitor in the main house, so there is no need for staff to sit it out in the kennels watching out for any prospective problem within the kennel block itself. They can monitor the situation from the comfort and safety of the house, yet they are still in a position to assist at very short notice. We have found this system to be invaluable on many occasions; it is so sensitive we can detect even the smallest contraction in the dam, and I have spotted a puppy's movement while it is still within the uterus.

Chapter Three

THE RIGHT BREED FOR THE JOB

Certain breeds of dogs have been found to be more satisfactory than others for training as guide dogs, and it is their physical characteristics that we look at in the first instance. The height of withers should be a minimum of nineteen inches, and the dog should have a middle-of-the-road body weight. Some breeds tend to mature much later than others, and we prefer those that mature by the time they are two years old. The coat should be one that stands up to the cold but is relatively easy for a blind person to look after. A nice even gait is desirable, so is longevity. Temperamentally, we look for a dog with average sensitivity, good concentration and low aggressive tendencies. It should be tolerant of other dogs and humans, easily domesticated, easy to train and responsive. It should be able to live in pack, as it will be kennelled for some time, and it must not fight or chase.

From extensive experience, the following breeds have been found to be the most satisfactory as working guide dogs in Britain and other parts of the world:

Labradors, German Shepherd Dogs (Alsatians), Golden Retrievers, occasionally Curly Coat and Flat Coat Retrievers, and some Collies. However, our greatest success has been with the Labrador crossed with the Golden Retriever and the Labrador crossed with the Curly Coat Retriever. Within these breeds we look for certain physical qualities in individual dogs. They should be of sound conformation, and any dog with a poor gait or a limp would be rejected. They should be typical of the breed, and dogs of very poor cosmetic appearance may well have to be rejected, because members of the public are not always very diplomatic in describing a dog to its owner. It is obviously embarrassing for a blind person to have an animal which may be a source of ridicule. Dogs should be free from gross hip dysplasia (this is dealt with in another chapter), they should be free from progressive retinal atrophy (PRA), and all dogs are checked regularly by specialist vets for this eye condition and for cataracts. It is obviously undesirable to have a dog with epileptic tendencies, although there are a few guide dogs that developed this condition and were able to continue their working lives under medication. There should be no predisposition to heart or respiratory defects or skin or coat disorders. Guide dogs invariably travel a lot and therefore they should not be prone to travel sickness, which rarely continues throughout a dog's life.

As the puppy-walking scheme developed during the sixties it became evident that we should concentrate on certain breeds and that puppies should be selected from bloodlines that had proved successful in guide dog work. I started to keep records and it quickly became evident that the Labrador, not the Golden Retriever or German Shepherd, was our best bet. I was still committed to finding German Shepherd Dogs to suit our taller clients and Golden Retrievers were still used, but the majority of dogs in the training pool were Labradors. In fact the German Shepherd has the lowest rate of success of the breeds we use, even though guide dog work started with the German Shepherd Dog. In the early sixties we had not established the right bloodlines to produce German Shepherds of the calibre needed to be successful in reasonable numbers. Another factor which hindered the German Shepherd was that training started at ten months of age because the puppy scheme was considered very expensive to run. Puppies were brought in for training at that time, regardless of the different ages at which the breeds mature, and this naturally affected the success rates. German Shepherds need to start training much later, and we eventually decided to bring them in at about fourteen months of age. Golden Retrievers are usually ready at one year and Labradors can start at ten months. Because of the limited training offered to staff and the short training times allowed to train the dog at that time – ten to twelve weeks in all, as opposed to an average of forty-three to forty-four weeks today – the first requirement of any dog was a sound enough temperament to survive the basic training. Consequently, the Labradors we were selecting in the early days were rather more forceful and perhaps a harder driving and more active type of dog that we like nowadays. Their mental and body sensitivity would both be lower.

One test carried out as part of their selection procedure at that time was the reaction to gunfire. At first we used a starting pistol and later a 4.10 shotgun. The standard practice when I first arrived at GDBA was for the gun test to be performed within the confines of the grounds, in fact in the runs, which had high concrete walls. I thought this was too demanding and unjust on sensitive stock, and was resulting is us losing many worthwhile dogs. I decided to stop it after I saw the first intake of puppy-walked dogs being tested by a senior training manager. I was asked to go down to the kennel complex to see the new intake, who were mixed with recently accepted adult dogs who had already been tested. There were probably five or six young puppy-walked dogs who had settled in nicely after arriving from their walkers a day or two previously. As far as I could tell, having seen them during their puppy walking, they were all basically sound puppies. The procedure was to bang the gates, and the trainer called them into the runs and immediately fired the gun. The more sensitive dogs found this extremely alarming, and five of them were absolutely terrified and were rejected.

After witnessing this procedure I decided to allow the dogs time to settle in their new environment and to test them for gunfire when they were out walking in town, once a bond had been established with the handler. I would first condition the dog to noise by banging billboards, clattering wastepaper baskets or bins, slapping my hand on the metal parts of a car and stamping my feet – all the time watching the dog's reactions. Eventually, the gun would be used, and if the dog was slightly startled, which of course many were, I was none too worried, and they usually recovered after being reassured. After a couple of times the dog generally took absolutely no notice. If it panicked or worried, and got progressively more upset after hearing the gun, the dog was regarded as unsuitable.

The Labrador we use nowadays is generally of a very easy-going nature, although to some extent its place has been taken over by the Labrador crossed with the Golden Retriever. We will, however, need to continue to breed pure, in order to produce future breeding stock for further crosses. It is interesting to note that on occasions we had pure-bred Labradors of brindle colouring. People used to say that the brindle was a result of mis-mating, but it is not. Our breeding programme has produced litters with yellows, blacks, chocolates and brindles all in one litter. Most of our Labradors now are far more sensitive and willing than they were in the early sixties. They are far easier to live with and have a better mental attitude, but this is only because we have screened and selected thousands for guide dog work over the last thirty years. As a result they are suitable for a much wider range of people who come for guide dogs than any other pure breed.

In my early days we were getting many Labradors from gun-dog stock, but they were mostly bred to be very fast with tremendous drive. These qualities, coupled with their use of the nose for hunting, and other characteristics suitable for field work, were really very undesirable in a working guide dog. Since then the pendulum has begun to swing the other way because, I understand, many gun-dog breeders are now going back to show-dog lines to get quieter dogs. The Labrador's friendliness can mean it is easily distracted by people and inclined to go off with somebody else, which can be a problem for a blind person. It is also an adventurous dog and is likely to investigate and use its nose, especially for any source of food. We all know that most Labradors don't need to be shown their food twice – it is there and gone in a flash. This can become a problem in the street or exercise areas where people may offer the dog titbits, or the dog may find food which has been thrown away as rubbish. To the average Labrador, this can prove a major distraction.

The majority of Golden Retrievers coming in during the early days seemed taller and darker than today's dogs. They were less responsive than some of those we see around now and were inclined to be protective, a characteristic we still find in many goldens. I had previously understood that goldens were soft, sensitive creatures – appealing, chocolate-box dogs who look as though butter wouldn't melt in their mouths. This is true of many goldens we select for training, but among those we have screened out were individuals who started showing signs of protectiveness, particularly over food, toys, sleeping quarters or even the best armchair, when put in a strange or challenging environment,

I remember an early male golden, called Biscuit, we had in kennels. He came in for testing as an adult from somewhere in Birmingham. He was a lovely dog and gave good walks when initially seen in his home environment, even greeting the trainer effusively when he entered the house. The day after the dog's arrival at the training centre, I was told by the kennel maid that Biscuit was aggressive and refused to let anyone handle him, which was very out of character. When I opened his kennel door I found him sitting in the middle of the floor refusing to move, looking very morose and wearing an expression on his face which clearly meant: "To hell with this place, I want to go back home." I thought: "Now what's the next move with you, young man." I didn't push him, I simply walked in and tried to encourage him to come to me, but he wouldn't. I asked for a bowl with some meat in it and threw chunks to him, and he still did not respond, other than by twitching his lips. At that time I used to wear a flat cap and I got it out of my pocket to tickle him under the chin, while I sat on the bed and talked to him to gain his confidence. It was just as well I used the hat as a precaution against being bitten, for in a flash Biscuit whipped the hat out of my hand, shook it savagely and growled menacingly, then threw it on the bed as if to say: "Do not touch me, or there is more to come." He was a lovely dog and was obviously very upset at leaving home. I eventually managed to get him out of the kennel without bloodshed by using a slip lead. Curiously, once he was out of the kennel he reverted to being the dog we had seen at home, becoming quite affectionate and silly. But each time he returned to his kennel he became very protective. Biscuit failed to become a guide dog, as the chances were that he would react adversely to each change of handler and home, so he went back to his owner.

Many of the good points of the Golden Retriever are evident in some of our best home-bred progeny who have evolved from good breeding stock with the characteristics needed for guide dog work. They are reliable family dogs that are excellent to live with, to take into town or to work in the country. We have some difficulty in developing sufficient flexibility and width in bloodlines within this breed, and we are still striving to improve our stock, but many individuals work well, and willingness in our better lines is now high. A few tend to get hang-ups about certain things, usually during the early stages of training or when they are being paired with blind people and going home for the first time. They are a breed of dog that can put the brakes on and refuse to work. Willingness sometimes dries up and, when it does, it is a difficult problem for a blind person to cope with. I have known animals that start working well again when a trainer goes to visit, because they know full well that there is somebody around that can deal with them. At one time a term used for this was 'stubbornness', but that is not a fair description. A better term is 'lack of generosity'. Golden Retrievers are intelligent, they know what life is about and individuals soon get to know what they can get away with. It is a breed that is easily offended and when their generosity or willingness is withdrawn, it can sometimes be difficult to restore. We do not have many blind people that come to us as natural dog handlers, although they may become adept once they have had a few dogs and gain experience. However, gaining experience with a dog that is inclined to withdraw its generosity when you ask it to carry out a task, is like living or working with someone who is unpredictable, and it is not easy to develop a firm and lasting relationship.

The German Shepherd Dog is a breed that attracts a very strong following, but it has as many detractors as supporters. We are forever being asked why we don't use more, and the answer lies in the type of work we demand of the dog. It is a super breed – providing everything goes right for it in testing, training, matching up with a blind person and the environment in which it is placed. Guide dog work in Britain

Guide dog 'Zorro'. Labradors generally have an easy-going nature.

Guide dog 'Laura'. We have established excellent bloodlines for Golden Retrievers.

The German Shepherd is a sensitive breed and needs time to adapt to change.

Guide dog 'Shelley'. Border Collies possess a lot of initiative.

Brood bitch 'Penny': a Curly Coated Retriever

A Curly Coated Retriever x Labrador. Note the wiry coat.

The Golden Retriever x Labrador cross has proved the most successful, combining the best qualities of both breeds.

John Wright Photography.

was established with the breed in the thirties, and guide dogs are associated with the German Shepherd throughout the world. The problem with the breed is not aggressive or protective behaviour, which is generally linked with the German Shepherd; it is rather that the Shepherd is a very loyal dog – it has a deep desire to belong to someone, and it does not take easily to some of the situations in which we place it during training and pairing. In the early days when training was started at ten months of age, these problems were exacerbated. The German Shepherds needed longer with a puppy walker to become more mature. At one time, as an experiment, we left them out until they were 18 months to two years of age, but this allowed too strong an attachment to be formed with the puppy walker, which often disturbed the dog when he came in for training. This, again, shows the sensitive nature of the breed. I am an unashamed supporter of the breed, having been concerned with it for over forty years. At present, I have five in my own home. They are all robust animals, but they are mentally quite sensitive and have a deep bond to different individuals within the human family pack.

Unlike the RAF, police, and prison service, we do not allocate a dog to one person to be trained and handled for the rest of its life. At Guide Dogs, any puppy, including the Shepherd, has to go to a home to be puppy-walked at six weeks of age, where it will obviously become attached to and take his place in that family pack. About a year later the dog will be transferred to a training centre where it will be kennelled with a canine pack and handled by a number of kennel maids and trainers. The average Labrador does not seem to worry too much about this and easily accepts the change. This is not true of the Shepherd, and unless care and consideration is given to him, he soon shows signs of stress and will deteriorate both mentally and physically.

Everything with this breed has got to be right. Once a German Shepherd gets upset and starts to decline, especially during the time it is not strongly attached to somebody, it is difficult to get it back on an even keel. Like all our dogs, a German Shepherd is matched to a blind person who may never have had a dog before. This can create another anxiety, because the dog will be training with that person in close proximity to its class trainer, with whom the dog will have built up a relationship. Yet it will have to give of its best with the completely new and often inexperienced handler, whose orientation and balance may not be too good. I do not share the common belief that most German Shepherds are one-man dogs. They will adapt to change, but it takes time for them to adjust and respond. All individuals of this breed benefit by having experience of staying in kennels for a week or so before they are five to six months of age.

One other problem referred to by our training staff is that the Shepherd's long-striding gait makes it difficult to match them to a suitable partner. As a breed they tend not to be too tolerant of handlers who are clumsy or do not follow easily. In my experience a nice Shepherd with a good handler is a treat to watch, but it is not easy to find the ideal partnership. Given the difficulties, I think we are doing extremely well in getting a success rate of 68 per cent with the Shepherds we breed ourselves.

We do not use too many Collies nowadays. At one time there were a lot around, and I believe the record working life was held by a Collie named Lassie, who worked as a guide dog in the Midlands until she was sixteen years old. Curiously enough, she died two weeks after retiring as a guide dog. Longevity is an important characteristic in a working guide dog, and much effort has been expended over the years to establish Collies more firmly in our breeding stock. Even so, they are not highly successful numerically, and we still have great difficulty in finding suitable individuals from this breed. They have high hearing sensitivity and can crack up if they are subjected to too much stress, particularly in busy city traffic. It is a breed with a high chasing instinct and strong eye contact with things that move. Trainers who are highly experienced with other breeds often fail with a Collie. The breed can also be too small and quick moving to suit most people. They also possess a lot of initiative, which means that you have got to be not just one step ahead of the dog, as with many working dogs, but about four, and it takes a special person to succeed. The Collie appears to have altered considerably over the years. In the early days we got many larger-framed and heavier-boned Collies that were rather more phlegmatic than today's type, and the former type tended to have a higher success rate.

Some unusual breeds of dogs have been tried over the years. One I recall, was a Pyrenean Mountain Dog. She was a lovely large bitch of about nine months of age by the name of Sheba. I can't remember exactly where she came from but she was a great attraction at the time. Like some of the Golden Retrievers of that era she was rather naughty. She had arrived in poor condition and had knots of hair at the back of her ears, which obviously gave her pain. When I attempted to groom these out on the second day after her arrival, she immediately pinned me up against the wall and meant business. Her behaviour was similar whenever she was told to get into her kennel, and on several occasions she threatened me and other members of staff. Curiously enough, she responded quite well to a small office girl who had very little knowledge of dogs, and because of this the girl was conscripted as a temporary member of the kennel staff. Nevertheless, we eventually had to send Sheba home. When I met her owner, I realised how much she resembled the office girl Sheba had trusted at the kennels at Leamington Spa.

Sam was another unusual dog. He was a Bloodhound crossed with a German Shepherd, and was offered to us as an adult in 1961. He was an unusual colour, basically iron grey, but he had the soft Bloodhound expression without the wrinkles. When he first arrived and was walked out of the centre he appeared a little perplexed about what was happening to him. He was loath to walk ahead and used to look round at the handler a lot, but he became more confident through being encouraged and walked on a long lead, and became quite good. He developed lovely deep concentration once he felt confident. I took him into shops up and down open and covered steps, showed him people alighting from escalators, went into lifts and noted his reaction to traffic. I checked him with buses and took him on to the railway station where, of course, there were steam engines instead of modern diesels and electrics. I checked his reaction to sudden movement and noise as these trains thundered through the station, and I was pleased and surprised by his confident attitude to approaching the platform edge. I well remember taking him for the first time to the bus station, where he created a lot of interest. During the second week, while we were on our way back to the training centre, I thought I could hear a noise like a low whine. I listened, and it was Sam singing to himself. It sounded like a whimper at first, but he wasn't upset. I think he was actually singing to himself for pleasure, and I started to encourage him. I shouldn't have done so, but I wanted to know more about this unusual behaviour. I would encourage him out front and as he put tension on the lead, as if in harness, I would start singing to him in his own manner. He would answer me and we would keep this going for a long time!

He was a super dog and mixed well with others. At the time we were not considering many males, but we had Sam because we sometimes got requests for taller dogs for special students. He didn't use his nose a lot, which you would have expected with his breeding. He was a tall, gentle, very sensitive dog, and he was easy to control. He wasn't distracted by other dogs when he was out working and he wasn't a chaser, because we checked him with ducks, swans, cats and goats. The goats, incidentally, were the property of the resident guide dog owner, and the milk from the goats was used to feed our puppies. Sam was kept at Leamington for training and was quickly picked up by one of the trainers, although they were beginning to prefer the puppy-walked dogs rather than the adults. The trainer had a very high opinion of Sam as a working dog. He was particularly impressed by the dog's trainability and ease of handling, his confidence and his willingness – and fortunately he made no comment on his repertoire as a singer. Sam eventually qualified, was given to a market gardener in Kent and, I believe, worked for a long time as a valued guide and companion.

I have spoken about the large numbers of adult dogs that we acquired in the early days that did not make the grade as guide dogs. The reasons were many and varied. The fact that we paid little or nothing at all for these dogs was one factor, but our advertisements failed to specify the type of dog we required. They did not state that the dog should have had a specially acquired early education and experience of town conditions. We did not stipulate that we were looking for dogs that had been socialised and were accustomed to the sound of the human voice. Basically, all our adverts said was that we wanted dogs or bitches of a certain age, group and size, which resulted in breeders and dealers offering us kennel dogs surplus to their requirements that had no experience of humans or town life. Many dogs had lived solely in kennels from birth and, of course, were totally unsuitable for guide dog work. Although I had bred and trained German Shepherds, and thought I knew a bit about most dogs, I was puzzled by the fact that a lot of the Shepherds from breeders and dealers were perfectly alright while they stayed in kennels. However, they became scatty, worried, anxious and suspicious when you started walking them out into the town to test them. Many animals got progressively worse. It became evident that there was a pattern to this: the dogs were confident in the kennel environment, but worried as soon as they were away from it. On the other hand, family pets offered to us were alright in town and stressed in kennels.

At the end of my first year with the Association, I was offered a young and very glamorous Shepherd dog from a young lady breeder in Yorkshire. I travelled to view the bitch and was delighted. She really was first class – about ten months of age and she had scored very well in good company when competing at a breed show the previous Saturday. Her brother, incidentally, became a very well known show dog called Grand Vizier of Evely. I gave our usual assurance that we would take very good care of the bitch, and we would return her if she proved unsuitable after the statutory three weeks testing, and we would pay an agreed price if she was accepted. I had driven a round trip of 400 miles to collect the dog in order to make it less traumatic for her than a long unaccompanied train journey.

I arrived back at the training centre in the early hours of the morning with my prize. I thought she was not only good trainable material, but also important potential brood stock. She waltzed into our kennels, ate a good meal, despite the noise from her kennelmates, who were objecting to having their sleep disturbed, and spent a penny. I played with her for a while, settled her to her bed and all appeared well. When I started to test her she showed some slight concern in town, but I thought this would wear off as she became more confident in me and the new environment. Alas, this was not to be. She was daily less able to accept town conditions, and one of our kennel girls reported that the dog had lost her zest for life. Her eyes became dull, she lost weight and so testing was stopped. We paired her with several new friendly Labradors, some Golden Retrievers and even German Shepherd Dogs in the hope of boosting her confidence. We gave her tonics for loss of appetite. Our vet gave her B12 and prescribed Spareen, which is a mild tranquilliser, in the hope that it would help, but to no avail. By this time she was eating just sufficient to keep her going. She had lost her lovely condition and looked remarkably like a bad RSPCA case. The situation caused us so much concern that both the kennel maid and I could have done with taking Spareen ourselves! I then decided the only tonic the poor bitch needed was to go home. I therefore rang the owner and prepared her for the worst, informing her that we had tempted the bitch with all types of food, including chicken. She was at a loss to understand what had happened, because the bitch had always been so good at home. She said: "OK, bring her back tomorrow and I will get my vet up to see her in case there is something more seriously wrong."

The next day I lifted the dog into my Hillman Husky, for she did not appear to have the energy or desire to jump, and looked very sad. On the way home I spoke to her continuously from the driver's seat, while she lay motionless in the cage at the rear. I was wondering all the time what the breeder would think of our approach to caring for stock when she saw her. As we approached the town boundary after the 200 mile drive, I thought the bitch was having a convulsion because she started to make an almighty noise, screaming and clawing the cage and windows of the van. No amount of vocal restraint calmed her. She had come to life when she recognised her home area and the pleasure could be seen in the way her tail wagged and her eyes lit up. When we got to the house the breeder came out to see her. She was a very kind and understanding woman, and although she was obviously taken aback by the bitch's loss of weight and condition, she was probably relieved to see that her animal was happy to return home. I thankfully accepted the offer of a cup of tea, so as to have the chance to talk over the problem. The breeder said the vet was coming later to see the bitch because of her loss of appetite. There was a wonderful smell of home-baked cooking as we passed through the kitchen, and there in full array were lemon curd tarts, jam tarts, sponge cakes and currant buns, all fresh out of the oven. I thought to myself, no wonder the bitch didn't like leaving home, who the hell would! About ten minutes later, after viewing a litter of Shepherd pups up the garden, we returned to see the bitch polishing off the last of the cakes. Needless to say, the good lady took me to task and said: "But I thought you said she would not eat." I could only reply: "Those cakes presented at our kennels on a silver platter would not have been acceptable to her. She is home, she is happy – and I am very embarrassed." My explanation was accepted, and I was later told the bitch quickly put on weight and was soon back in the ring winning prizes again. The bitch, incidentally, was called Cheeta – a very appropriate name.

Cheeta's behaviour is typical of German Shepherd Dogs that have been well humanised from an early age and developed a firm bond with their owners, but have not experienced, at the same time, solid conditioning to a kennel environment and town conditions over the same period. They lack the experience available to puppy walked dogs during the critical stages of their development. As the years have progressed we have narrowed the field down mainly to the Labrador, the Golden Retriever, the German Shepherd Dog and the occasional Collie. But one of the most interesting products of guide dog breeding today are the cross-breeds. These are the offspring of pure-bred parents whose family lines have been selectively bred over many years for guide dog work.

Among the unusual dogs that came in as adults in the early days were a number of crosses. Many kinds were tested, the best being Golden Retrievers crossed with Labradors. They looked more like Labradors, but they had rather thicker and denser coats, and were slightly more angular than the average Labrador. These crosses were exceptionally good workers and I saw others in dog clubs that also appeared to be good workers and very tractable. But to get the best value out of each cross-breed, it was clearly important to establish and evaluate the qualities and hang-ups of a number of thoroughbred family lines. I decided to cross the retriever breeds rather than Shepherds and Collies, because the retrievers had much more thorough proven records of guide dog work, and many more had qualified. Golden Retrievers had good qualities under certain circumstances, but because of certain problems in their make-up there was lack of willingness in the breed which was not found in most Labrador lines. On the other hand, some Labradors were perhaps a bit over-generous, somewhat bumptious and difficult for the more sensitive blind person to live and cope with. It therefore became evident that we ought to try mixing the two breeds together in the hope of overcoming these problems by pairing members of each breed, in order to enhance the desirable traits from each, and eliminate the undesirable ones.

We wanted some of the gentleness of the Golden Retriever, which was found in the better lines of this breed, and fortunately, even in the very early crosses, things looked promising. We were pleased and perhaps surprised when we found in those early litters there were some of the nicest, most malleable puppies we had seen for a long time. The experienced puppy-walkers with whom the puppies were placed all sent good reports about how easy these puppies were to live with, and how easy they were to walk and control, compared with some of the more exuberant Labrador puppies that they had experienced before. This applied to both male and female puppies. The reports encouraged us to continue the crossing.

By 1970 we were making progress with the Labrador Retriever cross Golden Retriever, and it became evident that even the males of these litters were far more acceptable and successful than some of the pure pedigree lines. At the time only some 20 per cent of the male puppies we bred were accepted into training, but the crosses changed the picture and enabled us to increase the supply of dogs going to the centres, thus reducing the waiting lists for a guide dog. Out next cross was a Curly Coated Retriever and a Labrador. We had a very, very good black Labrador stud, Ben, who was renowned for stamping generosity and willingness into his stock, and he was used on a Curly Coat Retriever bitch named Penny. The result of the mating was a large, good-quality litter, which was very successful through walking and training. We subsequently repeated the mating on a small scale, and we now have quite a number of cross Curly Coat-Labrador guide dogs. The last assessment showed that of seventy-eight forwarded for training between August 1976 and January 1986, seventy-four had successfully qualified as guide dogs, giving a record success rate of 94.8 per cent. At the time, I had not thought crossing would improve the coat, which in a pure Curly Coat can be a problem for a guide dog owner. In fact, the majority of these crosses have a wire coat, as opposed to a proper curl, which does not need trimming and still gives good protection against the weather.

I recall that after we had trained the first of these crosses two of our trainers asked me to breed more of them, because they found they could pair them with more elderly clients. For some reason, these dogs did not get over-worried or over-anxious if they were misunderstood, for want of a better expression, during early pairing with older clients, who had slower reflexes or bad balance. They would still plod on and do the job which they had been trained to do, without taking advantage and challenging their owners. This meant they could fill a gap which would normally have been filled by a mature dog which had been returned to the training centre, perhaps because his owner had died or was not able to use him or keep him for some reason. Since then we have crossed the Golden Retriever with the Collie, mainly because we have been unable to establish enough pure Collie lines which have produced good guide dogs. When the first litter from this cross was born, I was rather disappointed and wondered why I had embarked on the experiment – they looked a real motley crew. However, I think all but one from seven made the grade. Some worthwhile comments came back from the training centres and we have repeated the cross several times since. I should add that as adults they were much more attractive than as puppies.

Some breeders criticised us when we first started deliberate cross breeding. The English Kennel Club had just made a rule that they would not register inter-bred dogs of two different breeds, which created problems for us. The breeders understandably wanted to keep their breeds pure, and we did not want to upset them when they had helped us so much over the years. Initially any of our cross-bred dogs which were rejected had their pedigrees marked very clearly so that there was no doubt about their breeding. Today rejects from our breeding or training centres will, of course, have been either castrated or spayed, so there is no chance of breeding from them.

When we tried breeding a double cross, the sire being a Golden Retriever cross, mated to a Labrador cross Golden Retriever, the progeny tended to show over-sensitivity in heavy traffic areas, especially in big cities like London. This is one reason why I feel we should go no further than the first crosses. Their success is such that 50 per cent of our output are now crosses and they achieve a success rate of about 80 per cent.

Temperamentally, guide dogs must be stable, reasonably energetic and have a pleasing disposition.

Chapter Four

WHAT MAKES A GUIDE DOG

Guide dogs are destined to live a demanding and sometimes stressful life. They must be sound physically, but equally important, they must have the right temperament. They should be stable, reasonably energetic and of a happy, pleasing disposition. They should not be neurotic, shy, frightened or hyperactive. We have to check that they are not aggressive in any way. Low chasing instinct is a very desirable trait, as a working dog hurtling after cats, for example, could cause endless problems. The dogs must be able to concentrate and work with the minimum of distractions. Willingness is vital, because the work is based very largely on it, and any dog with persistent low-willingness will probably be rejected. It is essential that the dogs are confident with and tolerant of children and other animals. Response to the human voice is important and we check hearing sensitivity, so that there are no sound-shy dogs. Moderate initiative is useful, but it should not be too great. Although the dog has to make decisions, it is not desirable to have an animal that is too dominant. It should be adaptable and within certain limits of body sensitivity. Tactile and hearing sensitivities should be neither too high nor too low. Very low physical sensitivity invariably produces a hard dog, whereas high sensitivity will produce acute softness. Very low hearing sensitivity means a dog is unresponsive, and if it is very high the dog will react to the slightest sound.

Sensitivity to touch can be assured by measuring a dog's response to affection, such as caressing, stroking and patting, or correction through the collar, leash and harness. As all guide dogs work in public and usually for people with less ability to control them than the original trainers, dogs need to be responsive. Guide dogs will generally be in one of three groups:–

1. Slightly under medium sensitivity to touch, and medium sensitivity to sound.

2. Medium sensitivity to touch, and slightly under medium sensitivity to sound.

3. Medium sensitivity to sound and touch.

The first two groups will provide average dogs and bitches with the lowest reject rates, and they are easily trained by a wide range of trainers. However, it is members of the third group that, if well-handled, produce the best workers. They are what the hand-cut fine wine glass is to the heavy moulded glass: the former, handled carefully, will give long service and much pleasure; handled without care, it will crack and be of no value. I have already said that willingness is an essential quality in the dog, if it is to be trained and worked successfully. Demands in training may at times lower willingness, but a dog of the right calibre will adjust as he progresses. A good dog handler will detect loss of willingness and adjust his training techniques accordingly.

Many dog trainers and animal behaviourists believe that a dog does not have intelligence. My experience suggests that many do have limited intelligence, and that this can be seen in the dog's ability to learn and understand his work quickly and well. It is also closely linked to the quality of willingness. A dog's intelligence and initiative can be of immense value if it is used and controlled effectively. Equally, a dog may, given the opportunity, use this intelligence for its own ends. A dog with strong self-interest is therefore not acceptable for guide dog work.

Potential guide dogs are assessed for their capacity to concentrate. It is a quality which is usually not well developed in the younger animal, and it can be enhanced or inhibited by the state of health and well-being of the dog. All dogs are liable to be distracted to some extent, but providing the distraction is not excessive and can be controlled, ideally by voice, the dog can be trained successfully. Dog and cat distractions can be either positive or negative, and they can vary in degree. A small degree of positive distraction, provided it is not coupled with a strong desire to chase or be aggressive, can usually be dealt with by voice control to regain a dog's concentration and interest. Negative distraction, when the dog tries to avoid the animal it has seen, can be hazardous in guide dog work, particularly if the dog, through fear, requires a critical distance in order to feel secure. Obviously dogs with a marked degree of negative distraction would be rejected at an early stage.

The qualities discussed so far are part of the overall specification for selecting successful guide dogs. However, success can be influenced by a number of factors, and this starts with the feeling of security that a pup gets in the nest, with a calm, confident dam attending to the puppy's welfare. From three weeks onwards, the puppy requires regular handling to influence tactile sensitivity, and it must regularly hear the human voice associated with pleasure. A puppy learns to play with its littermates and to understand dog language, and it is protected from fear by the barking of its dam, which activates the flight mechanism in pups. Any barking directed towards humans by a nursing dam should be curtailed, because the human voice should, at this stage, promote pleasure. Separation from the dam and siblings at the early age or six or seven weeks, when the pup is put out to be reared as an individual, is important. However, this should not be attempted earlier than six weeks, as it can result in anti-social behaviour directed at other dogs at a later stage. If the puppies are left too long before making the break or stay too long in a canine or kennel environment, a critical stage of their development may well have passed, and their relationship with humans may never reach its full potential. I have followed the progress of some 24,000 puppies over twenty-eight years, and my observations indicate that from seven weeks onwards, the ability to be socialised recedes. It is therefore important that puppies who are to become successful guide dogs gain the correct and regular exposure to people at the right stage of their development. The aim should be to replace the imprinting of the canine hierarchy and social status so that the pup's attachments, experiences and control come from people. It is also essential that it has exposure to the urban conditions in which it will eventually work.

When the puppies are about a year old, they will leave the security of their homes to return to kennel-life, and once again they will have to live in a canine world without becoming worried, stressed, nervous, aggressive or neurotic. During their stay in kennels they will have to work with several different handlers, and they may not always understand what is being asked of them during their periods of training. At the end of the day they will return to kennel-life, and not to their home. This will obviously place some stress on them, particularly after a bad day, and willingness is therefore essential. By the time the training has been completed the dogs will have acquired respect and affection for their trainers – whereupon they will be lifted from pack-life to become, once again, individual dogs attached to new, blind handlers who, in the space of four weeks, will be taught how to use the dogs, how to control them, and how to gain their affection. During the next four weeks, the loyalty, affection and respect of the dogs must remain with the trainers while they teach the new guide dog owners how to use their dogs effectively, but this allegiance must be carefully transferred. At the end of the four weeks the dogs will be taken to their new homes to pursue the lives for which they have been trained. A successful dog will, on average, qualify at about two years of age, and should work for seven to nine years.

The performance of a guide dog during its training and working life is clearly a vital factor in judging the breeding stock from which it comes. The Breeding Centre therefore relies heavily on accurate reports from the training centres. The quality of a litter is determined by the success of all the puppies, and not by a single outstanding individual. For example, if we have a litter of eight, and seven are rejected and one becomes an outstanding guide dog, this is not as satisfactory as a litter of eight where all eight qualify, although none is outstanding. It is only by collating information over the years that we have steadily improved the product. The future success of our breeding programme will also depend on knowing of any changing trends in the characteristics of our future clients, because this will affect the specification of the puppies to be bred for work twenty months later.

Police dogs, working collies, search and rescue dogs, drug-detecting dogs, hearing dogs and tracking dogs are all using their inborn instincts – chasing, herding, scenting, retrieving – to achieve success, and their selection and training is based on this. In guide dog work we select away from these natural instincts, and we also restrict the dog's critical area of independence by attaching it to a human through a harness. The total aspect of guiding work goes against what the dog would do under normal instinctive conditions.

Although this chapter outlines the selection required to produce good guide dogs, it stops at the point where the dog meets its blind owner. It does not outline the equally searching procedure for matching the dog with a suitable applicant. It is, of course, the outcome of the pairing which establishes whether the dog becomes good, average, or even a failure. The ideal guide dog is therefore a product of good breeding and socialising, careful conditioning to the right environment, expert training, and matching to an ideal owner. The criteria which are essential for a satisfactory guide dog are:

PHYSICAL CRITERIA (All breeds).

1. Height at withers.
2. Body weight.
3. Age at maturity 1-2 years.
4. Coat.
5. Stamina.
6. Conformation.
7. Even gait.
8. Longevity.

TEMPERAMENTAL CRITERIA (All breeds).

1. Appropriate sensitivity – tactile.
2. Appropriate sensitivity – hearing.
3. Capable of holding concentration.
4. Low aggressive tendencies.
5. To be tolerant of other dogs.
6. To be tolerant of humans.
7. To be easily domesticated.
8. To be trainable and responsive.
9. To be able to live in a pack.
10. Non-fighter and non-chaser.

From extensive experience, the following have been found to be the most satisfactory as working guide dogs, nationally – and worldwide:–

Labradors (black, yellow and chocolate).
German Shepherd Dogs (Alsatians).
Golden Retrievers.
Curly Coat Retrievers.
Flat Coat Retrievers.
Collies.

Selection of the breed covers the physical and temperamental criteria given above, but when selecting individuals from an acceptable breed the following characteristics are necessary:–

PHYSICAL CRITERIA (Pure breeds)

 1. To be of sound conformation.
 2. To be typical of the breed it represents.
 3. To be complete – cosmetically.
 4. To be of good functional trait.
 5. Free from gross H.D. or Anoconeal Process.
 6. Free from Progressive Retinal Atrophy.
 7. Free from Cataract.
 8. Free from Epileptic tendencies.
 9. Free from any predisposition to heart or respiratory defects.
10. Free from any predisposition to skin or coat disorders.
11. Free from excessive travel sickness.
12. Longevity.

TEMPERAMENTAL QUALITIES (Pure breeds)

 1. To be stable.
 2. To be of happy pleasing disposition.
 3. Not to be neurotic, shy or frightened.
 4. To be energetic.
 5. Not to be hyperactive.
 6. Not to be aggressive in any of the forms:-a. pure, b. protective, c. apprehensive.
 7. To be of low chasing instinct.
 8. To have the ability to concentrate.
 9. To have minimal distractions.
10. To have good willingness.
11. To be confident with children, at the same time being tolerant.
12. To be confident with other animals, at the same time being tolerant.
13. To be responsive to human voice.
14. Not to be sound shy.
15. To have good initiative.
16. Not to be too dominant or have self-right.
17. To have the ability to change environment and handler without undue stress.
18. To be within the limits or tolerances on hearing and body sensitivity.

TEMPERAMENTAL SENSITIVITIES

The primary sensitivities which are assessed in a prospective guide dog are the tactile and hearing sensitivities, and these range from very high to quite low. In our screening of dogs we select within the tolerances along the medium range, rejecting the low and highly sensitive animals:–

1. Very low = hard = under-sensitive.

(Tactile)

2. Very high = acute softness = over-sensitive.

3. Very low = unresponsive = under-sensitive.

(Hearing)

4. Very high = over-reactive = over-sensitive.

These are the lines by which we shall train and communicate with the dog during work and in training, and the amount of response we get from this source will enable us to measure the effect of our teaching and will be our means of effective control.

TACTILE SENSITIVITY

Sensitivity to touch can be assessed by measuring the dog's response or reaction to:–
1. Affection: caressing, stroking, patting, etc.
2. Correction: through collar, leash, hand, harness.

HEARING SENSITIVITY

1. Response to voice intonation (negative and positive).
2. To have no fear of thunder, gun fire or high-pitched sound.
3. To have no fear of concealed sound.
4. Not to be hard of hearing or deaf.

The ideal animal here would be of medium hearing range, and would have the capacity and ability to detect and respond to commands of moderate volume. It must have the ability to differentiate and be stimulated or inhibited by the change in intonation of male and female voice, for it is through this medium that we shall effect our best teaching, and it is here that the visually handicapped person will gain the easiest and most efficient control.

SELECTING THE QUALITIES IN THE IDEAL DOG

No dogs are acceptable from the low or high groups. These are considered unresponsive, or over-reactive and unreliable. The desirable qualities in a dog are:–

SENSITIVITIES

a. Slightly under medium sensitivity to touch, medium sensitivity to sound.
b. Slightly under sensitivity to sound, medium sensitivity to touch.
c. Medium sensitivity to sound and touch.

From groups (a) and (b) we get our average dogs and bitches, with the lowest reject rates; these are normally easily trained by the widest range of trainers. It is from group (c) that we get our ideal dogs and bitches (that is, ideal in the hands of a good instructor and guide dog owner), for handlers of limited understanding and ability could easily spoil a dog. Success rests on the way the dog is handled. Inasmuch as we gain many superior workers from group (c), it automatically follows that it is here that we find most of our rejects.

WILLINGNESS

a. Low-willingness is a major handicap in training, and personally, I consider it unkind to put a dog of this type into training.
b. Willingness can and does fluctuate during the dog's period of training, depending on its ability to accept and understand its training.
c. These fluctuations can be inhibited or enhanced, depending on the trainer's ability to read the dog.

INTELLIGENCE AND INITIATIVE

A dog's intelligence and initiative can be of immense value, if it is used and controlled effectively. Dogs with self-interest and dogs with self-right are not acceptable for guide dog work.

CONCENTRATION

Dogs are assessed for their capacity to concentrate, for a dog with limited ability to concentrate would be of little value.

DISTRACTION

This is present in all dogs and bitches in varying degrees. Providing the level of distraction is not excessive, and the dog can be controlled by voice, then it can be trained successfully.

Chapter Five

THE BLUE PETER CONNECTION

Among the very many enjoyable experiences I have had during my time with Guide Dogs was appearing on the children's television programme *Blue Peter*. The benefits to the Guide Dogs for the Blind Association have been enormous, not only in the vast amount of money collected by the children, but also from the interest that has been generated in the dog side of our work, which has, year by year, increased the number of people who volunteer as puppy walkers and who care for our breeding stock.

My first contact with the programme was while I was still working at Edmondscote Manor, the Training Centre in Leamington Spa. One morning there was a knock at the door and I was confronted with a well-spoken lady who appeared relatively knowledgeable about dogs. Her opening question was: "Would I be able to help *Blue Peter*?" At that time, I didn't even know that *Blue Peter* was a television programme, but I was soon informed that the programme had recently acquired a puppy. Unfortunately it had died after just one appearance in front of the cameras when it was only nine weeks old, and they needed to replace it with a similar-looking puppy. I was handed a photograph, and saw a mixed breed, a Heinz variety of mongrel, and obviously we had nothing that remotely resembled this puppy. But by this time I had established from Angela Mulliner, the lady in question, that the purpose of having a dog on the programme was to show children how to rear a puppy, and she wondered whether they could rear a puppy for us as a potential guide dog. I replied that they would have to start off with a suitable thoroughbred puppy, but if they were genuinely interested, I would be delighted to help. At the time the programme's bosses were keen to go ahead with a mongrel, as they believed, quite rightly, that not every family in the land could afford a pedigree dog, and they wanted children from all walks of life, and all income groups, to be able to relate to an ordinary mongrel family pet.

About a year later in 1964, Angela came back to my office and said that *Blue Peter* were now very keen to take up my offer of a pedigree Labrador puppy to go on the programme. They had replaced the little mongrel with a dog, who was to become well-known and well-loved as 'Petra' – a true Heinz 57, who was featured on the programme throughout the fourteen years of her life. The plan was to launch a Christmas appeal on the programme, with the viewers collecting silver foil as a way of raising enough money to finance the training of a guide dog from start to finish. The appeal exceeded its target, and, in fact, enough money was raised to train two guide dogs, and to pay for the upkeep of a brood bitch.

I chose a nice yellow Labrador puppy from a litter out of our brood bitch Misty, to be the first *Blue Peter* guide dog puppy. The viewers chose her name – 'Honey' – after she made her first appearance on television when she was just seven weeks old. I took her down to the studio in Lime Grove and during the afternoon we had several dummy runs so I knew exactly what was expected of me and the puppy. The presenters at that time were Christopher Trace and Valerie Singleton, and while I found the whole experience of being interviewed in front of the cameras fairly bewildering, the puppy took it all in her stride. We broke for just an hour before going out live, and then there was a request for me to go to make-up. I thought they were going to do certain things with the puppy to clean it up because, of course, it had been fed during the course of the afternoon. However, it was not the puppy they wanted. It was me! I remember commenting to the make-up girl that she had better take off all the powder and paint she was putting on me before I went back to the kennels, otherwise the staff – or even the dogs – would get the wrong idea!

Coming out of make-up, there were a few minutes left prior to going live and I was amazed at the activity going on. Everyone seemed to be rushing about, shouting

Honey: the first Blue Peter guide dog puppy with presenter Valerie Singleton

Peter Purves with 'Honey' and 'Cindy', who both qualified as guide dogs.

instructions and wishing each other "good luck". Chris and Valerie were both very experienced presenters, and they helped me through the ordeal of being on television for the first time. I thought that the live show would be a carbon copy of the rehearsals, but in fact, there was a chance to ad lib, and I found, much to my surprise, that I was actually enjoying myself. When it was all over, I dashed home with the puppy to hear what my family had to say about my performance – only to find that the television at home was broken. It had gone on the blink just as the opening titles appeared on the screen!

This was the first of numerous programme items featuring Honey, as the plan was to cover all the stages of her rearing and training. One of the first films showed her walking in town and then being exercised in the park, so we could test her reactions to the hustle and bustle of urban life, and then test her on the recall when she was playing with other dogs in the park. The film director wanted to stage an incident in a shop where some crockery fell from a shelf, to see if Honey was startled. This was the first time that I had to request a change of plan, as I thought this could be dangerous both to the puppy and to others. As a compromise we settled on using empty boxes, which were pushed off the shelf – and Honey could not have cared less. For a subsequent film we took her on an underground train, gave her a test in town and then finished up in a church to see if Honey could cope with all the situations that she might encounter as a guide dog. Honey behaved admirably throughout, and the film ended with a shot of her lying quietly under a pew, while an organ filled the church with music. Honey qualified as a guide dog and worked for many years with a teacher called Elsie Whitehead, who appeared on the programme with Honey on many occasions.

Cindy, another yellow Labrador, was the second dog walked by *Blue Peter*, and life was made easier because I had a Puppy Walking Supervisor based in Maidenhead, so she could keep a check on the Cindy's progress. Again, this was a very straightforward puppy who presented few problems, and by now the whole *Blue Peter* team were very well versed in what we required. This time, I took the whole litter, including Cindy to the studio, as Biddy Baxter, who was the programme's Editor, wanted to show me testing the puppies with gun-fire. Naturally, I did not want to do this in the rehearsals, so I just clapped my hands. However, when we went on live, I used a starting pistol. I honestly believe that it was the presenters and myself who were more concerned about the crack of the gun than the puppies. They were busy playing in their specially built perspex run, and when they heard the first crack, they paused for a second, but by the time I fired the second shot, they were too busy piling into one another to show any concern. *Blue Peter* presenter Peter Purves took charge of Cindy on the programme, and this was the start of a long involvement with Guide Dogs, which went on after Peter left *Blue Peter*. Cindy eventually qualified as a guide dog, and worked with a gentleman in Market Harborough for many years.

The years went by and eventually Honey retired as a guide dog. She was kept as a much-loved pet by Elsie Whitehead and her sisters, but Elsie needed a new working dog. Biddy Baxter, Edward Barnes and Rosemary Gill, who were responsible for planning *Blue Peter,* were anxious to foster a sense of responsibility and continuity among the programme's large and highly enthusiastic audience. They therefore launched the 3B's Christmas appeal in 1974, and viewers were asked to collect buttons, buckles and badges to raise money to train one guide dog and to finance a kennel block at the new Training Centre at Wokingham. The response was amazing, and enough money was raised to train eleven guide dogs, to build one new kennel block at Wokingham, plus extensions to hospital blocks at Forfar and Bolton; in addition a new isolation block was built at Leamington, Exeter kennels installed an automatic drinking system, and an incubator was purchased for the Breeding Centre. The *Blue Peter* presenters at this time were Peter Purves, Lesley Judd and John Noakes. All three were extremely easy to work with, and they were all keen to get involved with the new puppy that was going to be walked by the programme. John, of course, had Shep, a little Collie which I had helped the programme to acquire, and this dog had so much bounce and personality that it became famous nationwide – it even had a pop song written in its honour. Again I took a litter of yellow Labrador puppies to the studio to select the *Blue Peter* puppy, we chose Buttons: named after the 3Bs appeal by the *Blue Peter* viewers.

By now we had developed a strong bond of friendship with the Editor, Biddy Baxter, and of course, the whole *Blue Peter* team. I always enjoyed the filming sessions, and on one occasion I learnt a lot about seeing things from the dog's viewpoint. The plan was to walk Buttons over Hungerford Bridge. This is a demanding environment, with the railway running close by and the river underneath. The crew set off with me along the embankment, and they had the idea of filming at Button's eye-level, so viewers would be able to see how the world looked from her height. When the film was completed, it was amazing to watch the sea of legs advancing towards Buttons, and it made me appreciate how much is demanded of working guide dogs in order to guide their owners safely along the town and city pavements. Buttons proved a first class puppy and took everything in her stride. We were filmed in London, going into shops and travelling on buses and in taxis. On one occasion she had to climb three flights of open metal staircase, which was rather like a fire escape. Many dogs would be terrified by this, but fortunately it presented no terrors to Buttons; she was a very confident and willing bitch. I was now based at the Breeding Centre at Tollgate House, and it was decided to do a film up there, with Lesley Judd and Peter Purves experiencing a day in the life of a kennel-hand. They certainly learnt a lot, though I'm not sure how much they enjoyed it! Filming had to start at 7am, which is the start of the day in kennels. I remember it was a bitterly cold day, and presenters and crew were shattered after travelling up from London. Peter and Lesley got dressed in suitable kennel gear, and the first job of the morning was cleaning. To their credit, both Peter and Lesley lent a hand, even when it meant using a pick-up shovel and scraper, though the expressions on their faces spoke volumes! The dogs, particularly the large, more ebullient stud dogs, soon realised they had a couple of novices in their midst, and they took full advantage by jumping all over them. We certainly could have done with the make-up girl that day – if only to make the presenters smell sweeter after their exploits!

The film director wanted to do a sequence showing Lesley taking a string of dogs down to be exercised in the grass runs. Kennel staff are used to taking four dogs at a time, all on separate leads, but I suggested that Lesley might find this a bit of a handful – the kennel staff made it look easy, but four excited Labradors take a lot of handling. They decided to have a go, and Lesley started off from the kennel block and had to walk about 50 yards to get to the grass runs. I think this was the first time Lesley had experienced flying, it was certainly the next best thing to it! She was jet-propelled all the way and ended by crashing into the paddock fence. Fortunately, no one was hurt, and it proved that the sedate guide dogs you see working in towns have another side to them. They have an abundance of energy, and they enjoy freedom as much as any dog. Lesley and Peter completed their day in the kennels, feeding, grooming and cleaning – and it made a very interesting and amusing film when it was shown on the programme.

The publicity that Guide Dogs got from being featured on *Blue Peter* brought us great returns in terms of fund raising, and equally important, it provoked a great deal of interest in the work of the Association. This was the turning point as far as recruiting puppy walkers was concerned. On many occasions we were able to appeal for walkers in certain areas, on the programme, and the problem of finding volunteers was over. *Blue Peter* was the perfect vehicle for us, as the work of guide dogs and puppy walking was presented in an interesting and responsible way, and we were rewarded with a far greater response from the public. It is a link that the Association will be eternally grateful for. In return, *Blue Peter* was provided with plenty of good programme material – so everyone was happy.

After Buttons qualified, my next contact with *Blue Peter* was when I received an urgent phone call from Biddy Baxter. She wanted me to find a Golden Retriever puppy, not for Guide Dogs, but for the programme. I had to swear to complete secrecy, as they wanted to present the new puppy on Blue Peter after their summer break, and they did not want the Press to get hold of the story until they were ready. By complete coincidence, I had been to see a litter of Golden Retriever puppies that very morning. I had selected one bitch, but there was another bitch that I thought would make out admirably as a *Blue Peter* puppy. I promised that I would try to get hold of the pup immediately, and Biddy said they would settle the purchase price later. I then realised I had left myself in an embarrassing position. I did not have enough cash to pay for a second puppy, and I had to convince the breeder that I had a genuine buyer, even though I could not disclose who it was. After some discussion with the breeder I said: "I feel absolutely sure you will be delighted when you realise what this puppy is going to do, but at this moment I cannot tell." She immediately replied: "Ah, you're the chap from Guide Dogs that goes on *Blue Peter.* I suspect it has a connection – is that so?" My lips were sealed, but it was enough to convince her that the puppy would have a good home and the purchase price would be honoured.

The puppy made its debut on the programme, and Goldie was soon a firm favourite with the viewers. When she was one year old, it was decided to celebrate with a birthday party for her on the programme. All the family was invited: mum, who was called Amber and was still owned by the breeder; dad, who was one of our stud dogs, called Angus; plus all Goldie's littermates, which included three males. I arrived with Angus, and I soon discovered that the highspot of the party was going to be the presentation of a cake made out of tinned dog food, complete with bone-shaped dog biscuits for candles. The idea was to put the cake on the floor and let all the dogs dive in. To my mind, this was asking for a punch-up, and there was no way that I wanted to be involved in trying to sort that out on a live television programme. The plan was therefore changed, and the dogs were given individual plates, but even so, two of the males suddenly let fly at one another, and I knew that if the first plan had gone ahead I would have been refereeing the best dog fight ever recorded on television.

This was not the only problem of this little get-together. Lesley Judd was holding one of the young males, and he turned out to be rather amorous with a strong instinct for the bitches. Directly in front of them was a lady holding one of Goldie's sisters, who was just starting to come in season. As the signature tune started playing and the cameras swung from the titles across to us walking on to the set, and this young male grabbed the bitch and started to mount her. I was the only one there that was going to be able to stop a mating taking place on the set, so I quickly grabbed the male, giving Lesley my dog, which was not causing problems. I took the young dog away from her, and discreetly reprimanded him, so he knew who was in charge.

Derek with Blue Peter presenters Simon Groom and Peter Duncan, picking out 'Prince', the fourth puppy to be 'walked' by the programme.

'Goldie' pictured with her second litter of puppies six became guide dogs, one became a stud dog and 'Bonnie' (second left) is the current Blue Peter pet.

Once we got on set we were able to return the dogs to the respective handlers; the bitch was placed some distance from her suitor – and the programme went on as planned. The viewers never realised how close they came to witnessing their first practical biology lesson!

To keep Guide Dogs in the forefront, I encouraged *Blue Peter* to breed a litter from Goldie. We mated her to Danny, one of our Golden Retriever stud dogs. One of our brood bitch owners, Mrs Wyndham-Smith, took over the whole exercise of rearing the litter, for she lived in Kingston-upon-Thames, which was close to *Blue Peter* presenter Simon Groom, who handled Goldie. The whole exercise proved very successful, and from the litter of five, two males – Henry and Prince – qualified as guide dogs. Prince was puppy-walked by *Blue Peter,* and was handled by presenter Peter Duncan. Prince was a nice dog with initiative, and Peter found some difficulty keeping him under control as he began to develop. It was therefore decided that Peter should come up to Tollgate to gain experience in handling dogs. We gave him Angus – Goldie's father – to handle, as he was a very easy-going dog. Peter walked with Angus in the grounds, and we showed him how to use his voice in the correct way in order to get response from the dog. All was going very well, and Peter was beginning to enjoy himself, realising that he had the ability to exercise control over the dog. However, he failed to appreciate that he was dealing with a very responsive dog, of good body sensitivity – a willing dog that was eager to respond. He then tried handling Prince again, while we created certain distractions. Peter did well, and then we did something which I felt rather guilty about afterwards. We gave him a very large robust German Shepherd stud dog named Tollmark, in order to test his ability to the maximum. I also arranged for the head kennel girl to take a brood bitch in full season into the stud shed, just as Tollmark was coming out of the kennel, handled by Peter. The dog spotted the bitch, and in seconds he was off in hot pursuit, taking Peter with him! It was a very tough test, and Peter realised that control was not as easy with all dogs. The day, however, turned out successfully for Peter, as he learned a great deal about handling dogs, and I know he presented a much better image on the programme when he was working with Prince afterwards.

Before Prince came in for training, we had a last film to see if he was ready. We started at Heathrow Airport, to test the dog's reactions as huge 'planes took off and landed. Prince behaved impeccably. The last sequence was at St. Martin's in the Field Church, in order to test Prince in a completely different environment. At one stage, the crew ran out of film, and there was a delay of some twenty-five minutes. I walked around outside with Prince, as I did not want the dog to get bored. Peter Duncan waited in the church, chatting to Prince's puppy walker, Betty Carver. St. Martin's looks after the tramps in its parish by providing food for them in its crypt, and much to his horror, Peter suddenly found himself being told to leave the church by one of the vergers, who thought he was one of the down-and-outs. Peter could look a little disheveled aftera busy day's filming – but that was the first time a *Blue Peter* presenter had been mistaken for a tramp!

Prince eventually came into the training centre, qualified after a short period of time in training and is still working to this day with Mr. Bates, who has appeared on *Blue Peter* with him.

Goldie was mated once again, this time to a different sire, Zeke, and produced a super quality litter of eight, again under the expert care of Mrs. Wyndham-Smith. Six of the puppies made valuable guide dogs, and one became a stud dog. The remaining bitch, named Bonnie, became the new *Blue Peter* pet, replacing her dam, Goldie, who left with Simon Groom. Bonnie, in turn, has been mated, and we used our stud dog Wilson. She has now produced a very nice litter of six puppies, and so the links with *Blue Peter* are as strong as ever. This is a relationship that has proved enormously beneficial to the Association, as well as to *Blue Peter*, and I feel honoured that Biddy Baxter, and now her successor Lewis Bronze have invited me on the programme so many times, and have been such enthusiastic supporters of our work.

Part II

Breeding, Rearing and Training

Chapter Six

THE MATING GAME

The strength of the mating instinct in dogs is clearly demonstrated by the ease and frequency with which they seem to copulate on the streets. However, the scientific planning of matings, and effecting a result, is not always as straightforward as this would imply. The GDBA's breeding programme is committed to producing hundreds of high-quality puppies every year. We therefore have to do everything we can to minimise the risk of failure. There are only a limited number of times during a bitch's life when a mating can be attempted, and it is amazing how quickly she goes from a young prospective brood to an old matron bitch who cannot be used again.

I am often asked whether there is any justification in mating a bitch in her first season. Bitches vary in the age at which they come into season, and a first noticeable season for some could well be at sixteen months of age. I would not necessarily frown upon a mating at this age, but I would certainly say 'no' when a bitch comes into season at six months of age, because she is still very much a puppy. The average age for a bitch to come into season is about eight months, but there are exceptions either way. They usually come into season twice a year on a six-monthly cycle, but this also can vary enormously with bitches over a period of time. Some brood bitches are on a ten or eleven month cycle, and others come in perhaps every three months. The shorter cycle usually occurs with younger maiden bitches and may be associated with a slight abnormality in hormone secretions. Eventually they seem to find a balance, and the bitch usually settles down to a regular cycle. Seasons can be altered, in some cases dramatically. I have known a bitch to be brought on earlier than usual, if she is run with other in-season bitches. On many occasions a bitch that has seemed a bit slow to come into season has been brought on by being put into kennels with other bitches which were in the height of season. Obviously, this solution is not available to a bitch that lives on her own, and I am often asked what should be done in this situation, if the owner is anxious to have the bitch mated. I believe that the right thing to do is to wait until she comes into season herself. There are artificial stimulants available, such as injections, which are supposed to be of use, and we have tried some. However, I do not think they are the ideal. In our experience, the results with injections in particular are erratic. The best thing is to let nature take its course.

Age is a factor in the length of time between seasons. To some extent, the older the bitch gets, the longer the interval between the seasons, although occasionally it may shorten. Sometimes bitches don't stay in season as long, and the optimum time for matings can come earlier, but there are no hard and fast rules in my experience. Many books say that the twelfth day is the best time to get a successful mating, but I can show that it is the seventh or eighth day for some bitches and the sixteenth day for others. I have also found that there can be a definite family link in the optimum time for mating. The best bet is to note the attitude of the bitch. If you have a mature dog on the premises, it is relatively easy to check by watching her reaction to him, and vise-versa. Another method is to stroke the bitch, put your hand down her back, around her rump and stroke down to the featherings on her back legs. She will probably start pulling her tail across and will show a willingness to stand by arching her back. This is as good a time as any to present her to the chosen stud. You can check the colour of the discharge, which should be starting to clear, and check whether she is fully dilated and able to accept the dog. A scientific way of testing whether a bitch is at her optimum time for mating is the vaginal smear test, which most vets carry out. Obviously, you must take the bitch to the vet at the time the bitch is willing to stand, but be prepared to return several days later if the first test shows she is not at the peak of her season. However, I still think that the more accurate way of assessing is to check her with a good stud dog, reading its attitude and assessing the bitch's attitude. Why not ask an experienced handler or breeder for an assessment of the situation? It is cheaper and more reliable than taking her to the vet. Alternatively, you can buy a microscope and take your own smears, and this is what we did. The rule of thumb on the normal length of a season and the stages it goes through is: a week coming in – a week in – and a week going out. This is only a rough guide, so do not take it as gospel. During my time at GDBA I have seen fertile matings occur on the twenty-second day, and produce good litters.

There are numerous reasons why a bitch can come into season and suddenly go out again. It may be due to a lack of stimulus from other animals, or even a change of environment. Suppressants, such as Stilbeostral, which was once given to counteract an unwanted mating, can also have an effect. We have strong evidence that a number of brood bitches who received this drug subsequently had very erratic seasons and were difficult to get in whelp. In a few cases, when these bitches finally came into whelp, they produced very small litters. I understand that Stilbeostral can shrink the pituitary gland and prevent it functioning properly. Cortisone is another product of which I am suspicious. It is well known as a season suppressant, but it was not generally recognised as such in the early days and was used by a good number of vets to treat brood bitches. Many of the pups on our puppy-walking scheme will be used as breeding stock and we now ask vets to avoid the use of cortisone on a prospective brood bitch. Another reason for erratic seasons is lack of the right hormones, and their production can be affected by viral or bacterial infections. It may be worth getting the vet to check for a possible infection of the uterus or vaginal tract. In the case of getting reliable smears from the uterus, I understand this can only be done when the bitch is in season, and time is required for the cultures to grow, therefore one might have to miss a season before gaining a mating after treatment.

A sensitive bitch that is in season may be affected by stress and other environmental factors, and if she is at home she is more likely to feel relaxed. Obviously the more relaxed and secure she feels, the less chance there is that she will give wrong indications of when she is ready for mating. A very willing bitch might be put off if the dog is too abrupt with her, or the handler is interfering too much. There have been occasions when I would ask the bitch's handler to leave, and then found the bitch has changed her attitude completely. Previously, she had been too dependent on her handler.

The correct handling of a stud dog is equally important. Before we had many studs of our own, we depended on using a lot of outside studs. One December my assistant took a bitch to be mated with a dog that we had used several times with success, but this time he was just not interested. This occurred at the dog's home two days in succession; yet I had been down on many occasions and found him to be a very vigorous and dominant male who needed restraint. The bitch was very co-operative, but the dog didn't really want to achieve his objective, and I thought they would still be there for Christmas lunch! In desperation I went down to try to find out what was going on. The dog was being handled by its male owner, although on previous visits I had always dealt with his wife. She had sometimes assisted, and the dog had always done his job. At first I drew a blank: the dog simply did not want to know, and appeared rather concerned about his owner. I discovered that the husband exercised great authority over the dog whenever he was out on regular exercise because the dog was a bit of a lad and showed a great interest in every bitch he saw. Firm control was therefore exercised by the husband, so much so that when the dog was presented with our bitch he was very conscious of his owner being close at hand. Once the husband left, at my request, the dog's attitude changed. He quickly mated the bitch, thereby demonstrating the importance of environment, stress, control, and the influence of the handler in the success or failure of a mating. One of our male German Shepherds loses interest if the bitch has to be corrected, or if she is too boisterous. He is an exceptionally nice dog with quite a high body and mental sensitivity, and his progeny have achieved great success. However, if you dare to admonish the bitch he is due to mate, he immediately indicates that he wants to go straight back into his kennel. Yet when everything has been right, he mates his bitches and produces nice puppies.

The general opinion is that it is better to take your bitch to the stud dog so that the dog is on his own territory. It may well be that a sensitive dog will perform better on his own home territory, but the same may be true of a sensitive bitch. The more sensitive the animal, the more relaxed it needs to be. I remember the case of maiden bitch that had been exported. A short time after her arrival, in fact before she had had time to understand the intonations of a new language, she was sent for mating, which required a journey of some three hundred miles. She was to meet a stud who had never been used before, and the intention was to mate them on a public car park. Needless to say, the poor bitch was quite hostile and uncooperative. The dog was extremely sensitive and simply did not want to know her. The vet's advice was sought, and an injection was given to increase the intensity of the season, but when the attempt was repeated there was no improvement and the whole exercise was a failure. The bitch was classed as a possibly barren bitch with poor temperament because of her attitude to the dog. The dog was assessed as useless, and possibly unwilling to mate any bitch in future. In fact, we had bred the dog and many of his ancestors, so I was asked for advice. I told the owner that they had failed to get the mating they so dearly wanted because they had planned a rape instead of a mating. In order to be successful they would need to place both dogs in an environment where they would feel relaxed, and with people in whom they had confidence. This, I am pleased to say, happened the following season, and the result was a successful litter. In the early days of the guide dog breeding programme we used a lot of rather

'Guidewell Voss' – an outstanding stud dog. He sired over 500 guide dogs and breeding stock, achieving 91 per cent success rate with his progeny, from many different brood bitches.

Brood bitch 'Carrie' still enjoying her puppies at nine years of age.

dominant males, but we soon realised that the progeny from these sires did not tend to make ideal guide dogs. We wanted the rather more sensitive and therefore more trainable animals. Stud dogs with these desired characteristics are not always easy to mate, however. I remember bringing a bitch into kennels who was very much overweight, but there was not a lot we could do, because it is very wrong to reduce a bitch's weight dramatically when she is in season and due to rear a litter. I wanted to mate her with Carlton, a big German Shepherd. She was a matron bitch and showed little interest in mating. Her sluggish behaviour was obviously aggravated by excess weight. I could see I was getting nowhere fast, but I noticed that when I went near the food room the bitch became much more animated, and the dog responded to this. It was like the reaction of a young man to seeing a pretty girl walk down the street swinging her hips. A brood bitch standing still, not doing anything, is not too attractive to many young, inexperienced studs, although an older dog has a better understanding and may not require too much movement. Seeing the reaction of this bitch to food I got some chunks of meat and threw them the length of the mating area. She gaily galloped after them, and immediately the dog came alive. He ran alongside her and after the fourth or fifth lump of meat, he got the idea. She had hardly got the fifth lump in her mouth before he was on her back, and by the sixth he had mated her. The male, incidentally, totally ignored the meat. His interest lay elsewhere!

With an inexperienced male dog, ideally the first mating should be with a matron bitch, who always takes well to her stud dogs and excites the males. A smallish dog does not want a very tall bitch. She wants to be of comparable size so that he has a good chance, when he gets on her back, of being able to hit the target (for want of a better expression). The dog can sometimes be helped by gentle handling at this time – but not over-handling, which seems to make some dogs forget that they have got to do things for themselves. It is difficult to assist a dog that is cautious or worried about you or the bitch, and the danger is that the dog can easily wear himself out before he gets anywhere. Under normal circumstances, the stud should be encouraged to allow the handler to drop his hand on him at any time and in any place, irrespective of what he is doing. When I say handle him, I mean his private parts as well. It is important to do this handling beforehand so that it will not come as a shock when you try to help him in the mating. Ideally, I like to see a young dog make his own play. I like him to chase the bitch around and achieve the mating himself, but I may stroke him while he is riding the bitch. I then put my hand underneath him, put him in place, and then step back. It is important not to disappoint or frustrate the young dog, but also you must avoid over-handling. Too much handling will mean that a dog will keep turning to you. I have had dogs over the years who will come and nudge me and say "Well, this is your part of the job!" Helping at the right time, and having a dog that is confident in you, is all-important in order to gain successful matings.

A bitch that does not wish to be mated can cause quite a few problems, and a very persistent male may need sensible control. If you let a thug of a male set about a sensitive bitch, who is not quite ready for mating – or maybe even one that is ready – you can put her off very severely, and make her defend herself. There are some family lines I know that hug the wall and make it impossible for the dog to get his feet across their backs. Sitting down is quite common: the bitch will sit down rather than let the dog attempt to mount. Yet the same bitch when she is at her peak and relaxed will, without any encouragement, start courting the dog, flag her tail, intermittently stand and show interest by smelling him. A vigorous dog should still be controlled, though this does not necessarily mean by physical restraint. An experienced dog handler can control by voice. It may be a good idea to keep the dog initially on the lead, and give the bitch time to breathe and let her move away from him if she wishes. It is totally wrong to hold the bitch down physically and let the dog rape her, although I have seen it happen often, even with professional handlers, where they fear their stud dog or show candidate may get bitten by the bitch. They usually tell the owner of the bitch to hold it down firmly and, of course, they give them the end that bites! I prefer to give the bitch room to move. I like to see what she is going to do, even if she does use her teeth. You can prevent the dog being injured by restraining him on a long lead or, if you are skilful, using your voice and allowing the bitch room to move away from him. Encourage them to play and have a proper courtship by stimulating them until she eventually stands. It may well be that on that particular day she is not ready.

If the bitch is at her right time, and she has indicated this by standing, flagging her tail and showing interest in the dog, but is still reluctant to be mated, you can exercise careful and considerate control by encouraging her to stand still, ideally with the owner present. Encourage the dog to attempt to mate her. If you have got a good dog that has been taught his drill and listens to what you say, and he is happy for you to handle him, then invariably you can make it an easier and less traumatic time for the more sensitive bitch. Manual stimulation of the vagina with the finger can be valuable on many occasions – just to bring the bitch to the receptive stage. This will pay dividends for you in the future, because if the bitch has a bad time and is raped, she will not look forward to it next time. If she has had a nasty experience, she will remember it.

The point was demonstrated by a nice German Shepherd bitch who had apparently been hounded by four Labradors for three or four years when she was in season.

They had attempted to rape her and she had been put off dogs entirely. She had never actually been mated because she was very hostile, and she was very successful in defending herself from any dog that came near her hindquarters. The owner of the bitch came to us because he had been told we might be able to help achieve a mating (with a German Shepherd, not a Labrador). We did eventually achieve success, but it was not done overnight. The bitch had to come three times to the dog, and we never put her under stress. The owner had tried to get her mated several times, and he was always advised to pin her down tight and not let her move. All these attempts had been unsuccessful and traumatic. We allowed her to gain experience and confidence by letting our stud ride her in the sitting position before subjecting her to an attempted mating, and gradually she became more and more composed. I chose a very kind dog who knew his job, and allowed them plenty of space. We did in fact, muzzle her at the optimum time, when we were about to get the mating, because she had been accustomed to using her teeth on the Labradors. The muzzle was taken off immediately the dog penetrated and tied, and to the owner's surprise she was very relaxed and sweet. He said that he thought we would never get the bitch in whelp. She had beautiful puppies with a nice temperament. Subsequently she was mated again with little difficulty, and it was interesting to note that her whole attitude to dogs, even when she was out of season, changed very much for the better.

Let us now look at normal courtship displays when the bitch is ready for mating. The bitch starts by curling her tail across her back, possibly at right angles, pulling it away so that her vulva becomes more accessible to the dog. The vulva itself is generally more visible than normal. There is a definite colour change, as the discharge from the vagina starts at the onset of the season, and it is usually red in colour. A lot of people say that a bitch will not mate and conceive if she is discharging red, but this is not correct. A dirty discharge, which is particularly smelly, indicates a problem, and veterinary advice should be sought immediately without attempting a mating. If the bitch is handled over her hindquarters down the feathering, she will immediately start cocking her tail and looking inquisitive. She will also arch her back and push on to your hand if you put weight there. Some flirtatious bitches will dance around any dog that is introduced, poking him with their noses and even pawing them on the ribs. They will often mount the dog and generally become very excited, nibbling him with their incisors. Several of our Labrador bitches from one line appear to grin at the dog and make vocal utterances. The dog himself will tend to salivate and start getting excited, especially if he smells a spot where she has urinated. He will show a great interest in the spot, licking it and covering it with his own urine. His courtship displays will consist of chasing around, running up and down with the bitch, putting his head over the top of her shoulders and attempting to get his foot across her back which, of course is the first sign of mating. If she is receptive, she tends to slow down and starts to stand, cocks her tail and allows him to go through with the act of mating or riding. If she is not quite ready you could have to wait a day or so, or just a few minutes. If it is minutes, you will see a progression of improved attitude, when she will stop more frequently, and start playing with the dog by licking his ears and prodding and pushing him with her forepaws. If this progression is absent and she is quite positive about turning the dog off by sitting down, or continuing to threaten him, call it a day after forty-five minutes and try again later.

Prior to any mating the dog and bitch should have had the chance to relieve themselves, and ideally, they should not have been fed for a number of hours beforehand. A male is more likely to regurgitate if he has had a recent feed. If the dogs have travelled, give them a chance to have a small amount of water, but generally it is better to let them have a good drink after the mating act. If the pair go through the courtship display and nothing much happens, it might be sensible to pack it in for a while and perhaps try again later in the day. I believe that you have a better chance of achieving a successful mating during the quieter part of the day, which in our kennels tends to be the end of the day when everything is shut down and the majority of staff have gone home.

Once a stud has penetrated the bitch his penis becomes engorged, and some owners are concerned when they see a rather large knot at the base of the penis. You cannot see much of the bulbus glandis, as it is called, until the dog breaks away from the bitch – unless, for some reason, the penis does not penetrate fully and comes out. The knot is a natural part of the dog's physical make-up and ties him inside the bitch once he has penetrated far enough. Some dogs have difficulty in effecting ties, and bitches sometimes have a shortened passage that does not hold the dog. In a normal mating, however, the dog penetrates and the bitch grasps the knot and holds him there. The duration of the tie varies enormously from one dog to another, and with different breeds. The average duration of the tie with Labradors is about twenty minutes, but could be much less. In the case of German Shepherds, I have known it last three quarters of an hour, even an hour, which is back-breaking for the handler, if you are having to steady the dog and the bitch from the knees-bent position.

Although I believe in dogs mating naturally, I would certainly suggest that when dealing with inexperienced dogs or bitches, you keep a steadying hand on both animals. You should be in a bent-down position, holding your arms underneath the bitch, and possibly holding her thighs back towards the dog. After penetration and copulation, you should hold them in position with the dog on the bitch's back for a period, after which you should put his front feet on the floor beside her. Then the

The male mounts the female.   *Chris Bradbury.*

normal procedure is, with the dog's front feet on the floor to the right of the bitch, turn his left hind leg over her back so they are back-to-back. The actual time taken by the dog to mount the bitch, penetrate and ride her is very short, but during this time there is an awful lot of activity. A lot depends on the type of bitch. Some are quite vocal, and some will even scream. This can be quite frightening, and it is not confined to maiden bitches. I knew one individual that, even after several litters, used to let fly vocally, whenever she mated. She frightened one young stud, who thought he had done something terribly wrong. He wanted to escape, but of course, he was tied. This was another example of the need, on occasions, for human restraint and control. Some bitches make a contented guttural noise, which tends to start as the dog is ejaculating and suggests that she is climaxing, and all is going well. It has always struck me as a very gratifying noise because you realise that the dog is doing his job properly and has probably achieved a good tie, while she is contented and singing a happy tune.

Sometimes a stud dog will mount a bitch and enter her satisfactorily, then promptly fall out! The bitch may have a stricture, or the vagina may be rather short. Generally, however, the problem is caused by the bitch failing to grasp the dog. There could be several reasons for this: the dog may not have penetrated far enough, which is often the case with younger stud dogs that are learning their trade. It seems

The tie: This usually last for about twenty minutes, though it can go on for as long as an hour.   *Chris Bradbury*

particularly common in sensitive males who seem to be too ready to take flight. They are not stimulated or experienced enough to penetrate sufficiently for the bitch to grasp them. A dog may also fall out because he is slow to gain a good knot, which makes it difficult for the bitch to grasp him. This seems peculiar to older dogs. When the problem arises, the first thing to do is to control the bitch – steady her, but do not hold her against her will, because if she is a willing bitch she wants to be mated; she just needs steadying so that she does not move away from the dog. Someone holding her from the front can push her back gently towards the dog.

When the dog mounts and begins to work he can be helped in various ways. One technique I have used successfully on many occasions depends on the dog being confident about you handling his private parts. Once he mounts the bitch she is gently held so that she cannot move away from him. She should be spoken to calmly and quietly, and told to stand. The dog then mounts her and, if he is not able to penetrate, his handler should assist him rather than let him work himself to a frazzle. This is done by making a circle with the index finger and thumb of one hand, say the left, which is then placed over the back of the bitch and under the tail in line with her vagina. The dog will then penetrate that aperture in line with the bitch's vulva. The male is then vocally encouraged to work himself and penetrate the vagina himself, through the hole made by the human finger and thumb. Immediately that happens, the right hand should be brought under his tail and the back of his legs to help him forward on to the bitch. If necessary, he should be lifted slightly off the floor to take a little of his weight. However, do not pick him completely off the floor to start with, although I have had success with that; the aim is to close him up on the bitch, at the same time ensuring that the bitch is held gently back against the stud. The handler's position should change once the dog has penetrated and is working vigorously.

One of the better ways to prevent medium to large dogs from slipping back out of the bitch is for the handler to move around the back of the dog and apply pressure with both knees to the back legs or rump, clasping his right hand to his left under the bitch to lock the dog firmly to the bitch. Keep encouraging the dog and stimulate him to work hard at mating the bitch. It is important to hold him for a considerable time after he has performed correctly and has possibly tied. Keep them together for the best part of four or five minutes, then gently explore with your right hand to see whether a tie has been made. This will seem a long time if you are holding a large dog, but it is very necessary. If all is well, the dog should be steadily allowed to come off the top of the bitch and allowed to stand with his front feet on the floor alongside her. He can then be gradually encouraged to lift the hind leg across the bitch's back to enable them to stand back to back, which is of course the normal mating position. A word of warning when helping in this way – make sure the vicar is not looking through the window at the time. It could cause no end of misunderstandings!

With most matings the fewer people who assist the better, but there have been occasions when I have needed three assistants to achieve a successful result, but not by forcing anything – simply by steadying and encouraging. It is not always necessary to turn the dog, and in some cases where you know that the male is inclined to slip out, the dog can be allowed to stay on the bitch's back or stand alongside her, if this helps. It really depends upon the size and weight of the male. You should not allow the bitch to take all his weight without assistance. Usually the dog passes semen into the bitch in three stages. The first does not have a lot of sperm in it, the second contains a high concentration of sperm and passes into the bitch along with the first fraction, which is basically seminal fluid to clear and help the flow. There is then a third fraction, the prostatic, which helps to carry the sperm up the vagina towards the ova. During this time, the dog is held inside the bitch, and there is no way a human can break the tie. We have all seen or heard of people beating dogs or throwing buckets of water over them, but this is terribly unkind and unjust. The dog needs time for the knot to go down, and then they can break naturally. It is totally unjust to discipline a dog or bitch at this time, in the hopes of breaking the tie. What is required is calm, controlled handling, reassuring the dog and at the same time controlling the bitch by calming her down. It is also important to try and keep them relatively still, to prevent them from pulling and tugging at each other, or lying down. The length of the tie is governed by the time it takes for the blood to go out of the enlarged knot in the penis, although the bitch also grasps the dog and therefore needs to relax. However, the common view seems to be that it is invariably the dog who dictates the duration of the tie. I have never known a situation where a tie can go on too long, but I have heard of one occasion when a bitch died during mating. Unfortunately the dog was still inside her and ice had to be applied to release him. I am pretty sure that it would have been effective, applied suddenly to that tender part of his anatomy.

I have seldom seen any injury caused by excessive movement of the pair during the tie. However I have known bitches throw themselves to the ground with the dog still tied, which is something you should try to prevent. Another thing you should watch out for is the bitch falling asleep in the middle of the act! I remember one bitch called Harmony, who was an artist at this. She was a matron bitch who knew what it was all about, and during a long tie you had to watch her carefully. She would start to close her eyes and sway, and you had to tell her to wake up, otherwise she would drop down on the floor with a thud. I should add that it is possible to achieve a fertile mating without a tie. I have known some studs with a notorious record for not tying with their bitches, and yet we have had progeny from them. Interestingly, some of the offspring were retained as breeding stock, and they didn't carry the same trait. Although we had some good litters, and some full litters, from these matings, we also had a fair number of smaller litters. Whether this was connected or not, I cannot say, for it is natural to presume that there would be sufficient sperm passed to ovulate the ripe ova available for fertilization.

Some maiden bitches are difficult to penetrate because they have a tough hymen, but I do not think it is the job of a lay person to try to break it. You would have to be very experienced, and I would advise the help of a vet; though even some vets are loath to do this. I remember the very first bitch I ever took for mating was a small German Shepherd who was immature, even though she was three years old. I took her to a post-war champion whose owner's husband was a vet. We didn't achieve a mating initially, mainly because the bitch had a tough hymen that wanted breaking. She took the bitch into her husband who dealt with it, and then the dog achieved a successful mating shortly afterwards, which produced puppies. I also recall a bitch that we tried to mate with several stud dogs. Her condition was good, her attitude was right. The dog was very sure she was ready, and he was dead keen. However, he achieved nothing except her wrath, which she manifested as aggression. Everything appeared alright until the dog penetrated fully, when she would turn from a sweet, affable co-operative bitch into a roaring beast that would turn round on the dog, determined to sort him out. Teeth would flash, hair would fly, and in a fury, she chased him away. It was such abnormal behaviour that I felt we should examine her to see if the dog touched something sensitive when he penetrated. On investigation with the finger, I found a very firm blockage, rather like a dividing bridge at the bottom of a human nose. It was quite tough with a very small aperture at each side. Of course, this was what the dog was coming up against, and it was creating a lot of pain in the bitch. Even when I investigated, she had to be restrained. She was later examined by two vets. One said there was no problem at all, but his partner, who came in at the time, was a pianist with long, lean fingers, and he confirmed what I had already found. I felt quite triumphant about it. The vet operated on her to cut the stricture, and she was returned to us. I had some doubts about mating her, but with the vet's blessing we did. She mated normally the next day without any hostility, and in fact, she mated normally on all future occasions. The moral of that tale is to make sure you have a vet with long lean fingers, if you have a bitch with suspected stricture!

It is very common to see the most placid of bitches raise their lips and show an hostile attitude during the early stages of mating, and I never cease to be amazed at owners who are shocked that their precious little loveable bitch can display this attitude. The tie in the dog is an unusual and almost unique phenomenon, and I am grateful to Dr Desmond Morris for his comments on it. He says: "For many years experts have puzzled over this function in the dog, and many have frankly admitted they can see little point in it. One theory is that it helps to strengthen the emotional attachment between the male and female. The idea is that by prolonging the mating, it assists in the formation of the pair bond. It is true that the male and female become closer after mating and experiencing the tie, but it seems highly unlikely that the often painful process of being locked together helplessly for minutes on end will in itself endear the dog and bitch to one another."

It has also been thought that the lock makes mating more comfortable for the male, a suggestion that could only come from someone used to matings between experienced stud dogs and pedigree bitches, where the pair are isolated from other dogs and calmed down by their handlers. Under such circumstances the male and female may simply stand together quietly until the tie is over, thus giving the impression of resting. Another rather strange suggestion is that the tie is a defensive device which gives the mating pair teeth at both ends, should any other animals try to interfere. But anyone who has observed a tie in a wolf pack will have appreciated that the tied male is in reality extremely vulnerable. There is little co-ordination between his movements and those of the female if a dominant male animal comes close. It has been claimed that the tie prevents semen leakage from the female, but why the bitch should be so badly designed is not explained. A much more acceptable explanation, in which I concur with Dr Morris, is that a prolonged tie is needed to complete the three distinct phases of ejaculation, already described. It gives the male time to produce the final prostatic fluid, which is pumped into the female's reproductive tract and activates the sperm already deposited there. The tie also stimulates peristalsis in the female (a succession of waves of involuntary muscular contraction), which assists the flow of the sperm to its final destination. It should be noted that the tie does not follow ejaculation, it accompanies it. Because human ejaculation is so brief, we have been misled into thinking that the dog behaves in the same way. The idea of the male ejaculating for half an hour seems strange to us, but it is not hard to understand why the process of canine insemination should be so cumbersome and protracted when it buys time to ensure the delivery of the sperm successfully.

What happens when the tie finishes and the dog comes out of the bitch? Firstly, she should not be encouraged to relieve herself immediately afterwards. Put a lead on her and take her for a gentle walk, but dissuade her from spending a penny. She will naturally want to clean herself and normally, that should be allowed. But beware, because the next thing after cleaning is usually wanting to relieve herself.

The dog will invariably turn around and clean himself up, and usually at this time the knot is evident. He will lick himself to assist the return of the penis within its sheath. A point to watch is that some dogs have difficulty in getting the knot back into the sheath. It can be quite traumatic and, in some cases, painful. If a young male has this problem, it is important to let the vet see the dog. Occasionally the sheath can be tailored and a 'V' will be put in it, rather like widening trousers, but many vets do not like doing this operation. It is not usually necessary, and I have seen dogs in which an initial difficulty disappears after a few matings because the sheath stretches naturally. It is only if the problem persists and causes the dog trauma that advice should be sought. Some people advise dousing the penis with cold water, but I would be very loath to do this. However, it may be possible, if you are able to handle those parts of the dog, to assist him in getting the penis back. Sometimes hair is trapped when the knot is going back, and small amounts of lubrication like petroleum jelly or baby oil will help ease it back.

I am often asked how quickly a mating can be repeated. I have seen a dog go back within the hour and be vigorous, but it is better to give the dog a good rest in between. It would take an exceptional dog to go back in sixty minutes or so and be successful, after having a good mating. If the stud is a good one and was in great demand, I would have no qualms about using him three days on the trot, but I would want him to rest after that for several days. To ensure success, I strongly advise repeating the mating within a couple of days. Our excellent track record stems from this. In the early stages of our breeding programme we mated a bitch once only, and the conception rates were generally miserable. When we started doing two matings with forty-eight hour intervals, we increased our conception rates dramatically. If the bitch has just been on the verge of ovulating, she will certainly have done so forty-eight hours later. If the dog covers the bitch within forty-eight hours, you are certainly going to have a better chance of getting a conception and possibly a fuller litter. We have certainly been lucky in having relatively full litters. Litter-size depends mainly on the number of ova shed, rather than on there being enough sperm to fertilise all the ova that are shed. However, if the bitch is just starting to ovulate, the sperm from one mating may die off before meeting all the ova. A second mating forty-eight hours later could well catch the other ova that have ripened. It is quite possible for a bitch to conceive by more than one dog in the same season. She could have ovulated say at 12 midnight and mated at five minutes past. At that time only a few ova would have been ripe and come down to be fertilised by the sperm. More ripe ova would be shed during the next forty-eight hours, and if another male then mates her she could whelp puppies sired by two different dogs in the one litter.

There are notable differences in the ease of mating dogs of different breeds and temperaments. At Guide Dogs we are now confidently dealing with dogs that have been humanised and socialised from an early age, but in the early stages we took breeding stock or used dogs from outside that did not have these advantages, and they were more difficult to handle at mating time. A dog that has lived with humans may not understand exactly what you are asking it to do, but it does understand the intonation of your voice and whether you are pleased or displeased. This enables you to get the right reaction, which invariably assists any mating.

Many people, especially pet owners, feel that once their dog has been used at stud, it will become randy and attracted to all bitches. If a dog has been used a number of times at stud, he certainly knows what it is all about. But even if he has never experienced a mating, he still has the instinct and sexual drives, and if he gets in the vicinity of a bitch in full season, he will soon learn what it's all about. If you own a dog that is used sensibly at stud and is educated properly, you should still be able to take him near bitches (even when they are in season). He may get wind of an interesting bitch, but you should be able to control him. You must let him know through contact that he is with you, and he is not required to mate the bitch which he has detected. I saw dogs being controlled in this situation in the late forties when I became a member of the First Yorkshire ASPADS. This was a club in the Otley area,

Line-up of stud dogs at Tollgate House, proving the success of training and socialization.

close to Leeds, which had been formed by a group of top obedience and working trial enthusiasts who wished to advance their own dogs. Although members had both dogs and bitches, at no time were bitches dissuaded from coming to the club to practise and train (even if they were in season). In fact, they were welcomed by the owners of the trained males. This was because it was not unusual for members to attend a show where bitches in season could be shown in breed classes, and they wanted their dogs to be under full control at all times. This was done for many, many years, and the only exception was at competition time when the dogs went on the field first and the bitches afterwards. Having seen this in practice, I realised that, with good control, a dog can be both competitive and companionable – for many of the males in that club were virile, vigorous stud dogs, yet they trained and worked well alongside bitches, many of which were in full season.

Another interesting example was a guide dog called Guidewell Naturalist, who was a German Shepherd. He was an entire male and had escaped being castrated when becoming a guide dog. In fact, I got special permission to put him out as an entire dog because he was a very valuable and well-bred dog. We could have done with him as a stud dog, but at the time we could not afford keep him, due to a shortage of Shepherd dogs for training. I therefore got permission to put him out as an entire dog, in case we might want to use him at a later date, even though GDBA official policy was that every trained male dog should have been castrated. Unknown to the training people, on the day he was to be issued to a blind person I nipped over to the centre in the early morning and took Naturalist back to my home nearby and mated him to a suitable bitch. He achieved a good mating the first time although, in fact, it was the only time he had ever had a bitch. But he very quickly got the message, and the result was a very good litter. Immediately after the mating he went back to the centre and by 11 o'clock the same morning was issued to his new owner. I understand he worked successfully as a guide dog for many years. I should emphasise that although he was basically a very masculine dog, he was also very tractable, and with a good handler and a good trainer he was a good worker, despite his experience of mating. However, I would not recommend this as a regular practice. It was a one-off situation for special reasons.

If a pet owner has a complete male who tends to be rather randy and is inclined to fall in love with the family furniture, I would have no qualms about having him castrated, if he is not required for breeding. At one time I would have hesitated to say this, but I have now seen so many castrated males who have lived a very happy life that I no longer have any doubts. Many dogs which have developed unfortunate habits, and have finished up as problem dogs, sometimes even becoming dangerous, might well have lived a happy life, giving their owners a lot of pleasure, if they had been castrated at the right stage.

Mating a bitch two seasons in succession is a very controversial subject. At GDBA we would do it if the bitch's season was on a ten-month cycle or more; we would then mate her for two seasons and rest her on the third. A bitch on a six-month cycle would always be mated on alternate seasons. I suppose there may be special circumstances which would make us think of mating her on occasions other than that, but it would only be because she was an exceedingly valuable animal from a family line that had died out or was very small in numbers and ageing, or if she had had a litter of two and one had died. The next time she came in season, we might mate her again in the hope that she might produce a full litter and allow us to get the line more firmly established. The line could be lost altogether if we took the risk of waiting a further year, as she may well have passed away. That in fact did happen on one occasion. I was keeping two dogs, one as a brood and the other as a stud, as it was the last litter from a dog that had given us excellent stock. We had them puppy-walked for the first twelve months, but unfortunately before I could breed from the bitch, she was killed by a car swerving on to the pavement. If I had not postponed the decision to mate, but bred from her at the earliest opportunity we would have had progeny to carry on from her. Now we can only depend on the male line.

Incidents like this make you realise that there can be exceptional circumstances which should be taken into consideration.

When is the right time to stop breeding from a bitch? I have bred from a nine-year-old bitch, even some ten-year-olds. In the guide dog breeding programme, a bitch will usually be over two years old when she has her first litter for us. Those puppies will usually be about two before they start working as guide dogs, so you will see the brood bitch will be at least four before her first progeny start to indicate their true potential as working stock. Even then, you are judging from only one litter. You should already have another litter on the way, but by the time they qualify as guide dogs the bitch will be five years old. It may well be that the second litter is by a different sire, and that it turns out better than the first, so she is going to be seven or eight years old by the time puppies from a repeat of the second mating go through training. It is at this stage you have to decide whether to keep any as breeding stock. If you have done the right thing and the genetic pool is giving you consistency, then at nine years you are breeding from her in the hope of getting your future breeding stock. If she is good, then you want them in abundance.

Everything, of course, depends upon the attitude and condition of the bitch. If she hates having puppies or has difficulties in having them, then you don't breed, irrespective of age. I have sometimes rejected a brood of three or four years of age because she disliked having puppies or had great difficulty, even though the line she belonged to was of consistent high quality, and she had every chance of producing very good stock for a number of years. If, however, the bitch enjoys her litters, and I have known lots of broods who at nine love rearing puppies and are super mums, then I would have no hesitation in breeding from a matron of this age. However, GDBA has the best facilities that can be offered. We sit up with every bitch while she whelps, and there is a vet on call twenty-four hours a day. Therefore, the bitch is never put through any trauma or be placed at risk. With two hundred breeding bitches, we are in a position to foster or supplement feeds if necessary, and vital expensive life-saving equipment is on site, such as facilities for operating and incubation.

Unless there is a special reason, I do not see any justification for neutering a brood once she has finished her working life. We generally allow them to stay intact right to the end of their lives. When an animal is regularly bred from, there seems to be less chance that she will develop growths and tumours. I don't know that this could be proved scientifically, but certainly very few of our bitches have had these problems after retirement. Perhaps the very fact that they have gone on breeding to a good age indicates they have been fit and healthy bitches with the potential to maintain this condition to the end. This has been equally true of our stud dogs.

Chapter Seven

ARTIFICIAL INSEMINATION

Artificial insemination involves the collection of semen from a dog and its subsequent introduction into the bitch, often by means of a long pipette and syringe. The first documented case of a bitch producing live offspring following insemination with frozen semen occurred as early as 1696. By the end of the 18th century, Abbe Spallanzani was conducting research into methods of A.I. In 1955 a litter of puppies was born at the Canine Research Centre at Newmarket from semen that was then sixty hours old and had been transported from London by road and rail. In 1956 a Beagle bitch was inseminated at Cornell University, New York, by semen that was 140 hours old and had been flown from Great Britain.

Some twenty years ago it became evident to me that if we were going to keep detailed records to help build up our breeding stock it would be to our advantage to collect semen from successful studs and have it stored for the future. I started reading up on the subject, but at that time there was little that was being done in the dog world to collect and store semen. However, in the USA a Professor Seager had done a certain amount of research and had published accounts of it, and his work fired my enthusiasm.

I arranged to get help initially through the Milk Marketing Board's bovine freezer unit, which was quite close to us at Northampton. Every possible support and encouragement was given to us by one of their technicians, John Mawby, and their veterinary surgeon, who liaised with our own vet, Dick Lane. As a result, first collections were taken while I was still at Leamington Spa Training Centre, before moving to the new Breeding Centre, Tollgate House, in 1970. Collections were carried out early in the morning so that we could get the semen across to Northampton to be frozen within the day. We had to start very early in the morning, as semen was taken from three stud dogs. To do this we had to acquire an artificial vagina, or, to give it its full name, a Harrop's Canine Artificial Vagina. We later called it the Harrogate Waterworks. The device consisted of an outer rubber casing with latex liner, the space in between being filled with warm water. It was pulsated by an attached rubber-bladder hand-pump. I found that it required a great deal of time to prepare it for use because the water had to be at exactly the right temperature, which was 101F – the blood temperature of a dog. The water was actually trapped in the latex rubber sleeve.

The next problem was how to stimulate the male. Once we had the device at the right temperature, we needed to have a teaser bitch, and so we had to ensure that we had a bitch available that was fully in season and able to stimulate the dog to achieve an erection. The collection had to be done carefully because the dog ejaculates in three separate fractions, the sperm-bearing fraction being the second. The ejaculation of the first fraction usually takes between thirty and fifty seconds and the volume may vary between 0.25 and 5 mls. It is a clear watery fluid which contains no sperm. The second fraction, which is white and viscous, is the sperm-bearing fraction. The volume may vary from 0.5 to 3.5 mls and is ejaculated within fifty to ninety seconds. The third fraction is a clear, watery prostatic secretion, which contains no sperm. This fraction may vary considerably in volume, from 2 to 30 mls, and is ejaculated within five to thirty-five minutes. The three fractions were normally kept separate by collecting each one in a different test tube as it was released. The sperm-bearing fraction was then evaluated under a microscope which we had on site. Great care had to be taken to ensure that the test tubes were sterile, and they had to be the same temperature as the dog, 101F, otherwise the sperm could be killed. We also had to ensure that the sample was not handled with cold hands. Test tubes were primed with a measured quantity of diluent at the correct temperature, then corked, placed in a fridge and taken down to 5F above freezing.

They were later wrapped in latex rubber, packed in a vacuum flask full of ice and dispatched post-haste to the Milk Marketing Board for freezing down. We did this exercise many times before finally being successful with the sperm from one dog. It was successfully frozen and then, within hours, it was reconstituted and found to be living.

Using the artificial vagina was a bit of a nightmare, mainly because it leaked water all over the place (hence the name Harrogate Waterworks). If the water mixed with the semen it killed the sperm. Collecting semen into the artificial vagina from a vigorous male at the height of excitement was reminiscent of scenes from a rodeo show. If the test tubes were not at the right temperature or became chilled by being put on the floor, difficulties were created. It was altogether a very tricky exercise, and eventually we decided that the best way was to dispense with the artificial vagina and collect into a latex funnel which emptied into a test tube. As before, the sample had to be kept at the right temperature, taken immediately to be mixed with the diluent and cooled to 5F above freezing, before being put in a flask and dispatched to the Milk Marketing Board for freezing. In time, we became more skilful and 50 per cent of the samples were being successfully frozen.

Keeping the fractions separate still created problems. You needed to act very quickly to unclip one test tube from the end of the latex funnel and slip another on. With the stud treading the teaser bitch, the task might be compared with getting grit out of a friend's eye while you are both on the big dipper. We were also experimenting with various dilution rates at the time, but the crucial factor always seemed to be temperature. Resting the second test tube with the sperm-bearing fraction on the top of a cold sink top could kill the sperm off – or, at least, enough of it to make it less viable for freezing. Nowadays it is much easier to keep the sperm alive: we now have a heated water tank which keeps the test tube at exactly 101F.

Initially we stored the semen with the Milk Marketing Board at Northampton, and when they moved to new premises in Buckinghamshire they continued to offer us this facility. The semen is stored in large flasks of liquid nitrogen at temperatures as low as 320 F below zero. We are now making the first moves to store the semen ourselves at our Breeding Unit at Tollgate House. This has become possible since we built a new mating room with its own special clinic at the back, and we have been very fortunate in having a flask donated by two members of the Milk Marketing Board. Semen was not immediately stored in it because it is vital that the liquid nitrogen in the flask is always kept at the right level, and, to avoid disaster, topping-up routines had to be set up and tested before valuable semen, some of it twenty years of age, was transferred to the flask.

We have tried storing the semen in three different forms. At first it was stored in ampules, or small glass bottles. Very little was stored in this way, but we still have three viable ampules left from one dog. We then progressed to storing the semen in pellet form. This was done by dropping small amounts of the diluted sample, using a pipette, on to dry ice (frozen carbon dioxide) into which indentations had been made with a special tool. The semen was immediately transformed into frozen pellets, which were cushioned by the carbon dioxide gas released by the dry ice in contact with the warmer air. The pellets were stored within a flask in little containers, and we have quite a number of these. The final and current method is to store semen in thin straws; a practice which is used in the storage of bovine semen.

Inseminating the bitch with stored semen is effected with special equipment. Perhaps the most up-to-date kit has been devised by the French. It contains a long inseminating tube, the end of which can be inflated by a 10cc syringe to imitate the bulbus glandis of the dog. A second syringe is used to release the semen. The equipment reproduces the natural effect of the tie, the semen being sucked in with the help of peristalsis or vibration of the bitch's vaginal tract. To date, we have not attempted many matings using frozen semen because of the value of the stored product. I have to admit that we have so far had no success with it. On the other hand, we had achieved as high as 75 per cent success with artificial insemination using unfrozen semen that we collected from the dog and placed immediately in the bitch. This success rate is comparable with normal mating.

The value of perfecting A.I. is immense. Take the example of a useful dog that has produced good results over the years with many bitches. When he is coming to the end of his breeding career you may want to mate him to certain bitches that are a bit frigid, even though they are ready for mating. Rather than wear the old lad out and possibly not achieve a mating, it is better to collect his semen without tiring him, and place it in the bitch. In this way you will gain a valuable litter that you might otherwise have lost. I should add that we have only used A.I. for cross-bred matings, mainly because we have not wished to contravene Kennel Club rules regarding the register of pedigree stock bred from A.I. The Kennel Club will allow registration of puppies bred by A.I. under certain circumstances, but there is some resistance to it. We therefore use it only on cross-bred matings because, of course, these are not registered. Eventually we hope to use semen from pure-bred sires, who proved their potency in their lifetime, thus preserving and extending their genetic potential over many more years.

One of the reasons for our lack of success with frozen semen has been our reluctance to use up the limited amounts from well-proven sires. If we had been able to collect and store from established young dogs on the premises over the years, we could well have made more progress, because we would have had more material with which to develop techniques. I have a feeling that, unlike bovine A.I., it will not be one straw and one insemination. We may need to use all the semen from as many as three ejaculations taken from young virile studs in order to gain full litters. Further work may also be needed to improve the flow of semen when it is introduced into the bitch: we need to find a better diluent or to store seminal fluid to help the process. At present, GDBA has semen stored from at least ten dogs covering a mixture of breeds; the longest-living semen has been stored for 20 years.

I recall one occasion when I collected a flask, brought it across to the Breeding Centre and left it overnight for the insemination which was to take place the next morning. The bitch was checked, smears taken, the attitude of a chosen stud noted. There was every indication that the bitch was ready to receive the dog, so I drew the first canister of semen out of the flask. To my surprise the label indicated that it held the semen from three North American bison. A fleeting thought crossed my mind, because at that time there was a big demand for larger dogs at training centres! However, sanity prevailed and the next tube from the flask contained the right semen. If I had been less vigilant, GDBA could have made the *Guinness Book of Records* with progeny from that cross...

In search of further knowledge about A.I., I attended a seminar in the United States held at the Guiding Eye in New York State. Among the many people I met was a veterinary surgeon called Johnson, who told me of a scene he witnessed at the University where he studied. One day, he and his classmates went to the local bull farm for a practical lesson in collecting semen, using an artificial vagina with a teaser cow on a virile young bull. They had gone through all the techniques in theory in the classroom, and each man had been assigned a position to take up when the collection began in the cowshed.

Johnson himself had to go underneath the bull and, when it mounted, he had to place its penis in the artificial vagina. Cartwright was in charge of the electrical vibrator attached to the artificial vagina, and he was the man responsible for controlling the flow of current from the regulator. He had placed this machine on the floor underneath the teaser cow within easy reach of the two-pin plug. Behind both animals, assisting the bull into position on the teaser cow's back, was McKinley, who also had to ensure that the cow's tail was out of the way. The bull mounted with great gusto, and Cartwright switched on the apparatus after Johnson had screamed at him to get the thing into action. It was a disaster. Johnson had managed to place the bull's penis in the artificial vagina, but no vibration took place and the bull dismounted. Several attempts were made, and the same thing happened. Eventually the plug was taken out of the socket and investigated to ensure that the wiring was correct. Once again they tried. With a great roar the bull mounted, Johnson did his

All bitches are subjected to a vaginal smear test to establish the time of ovulation and maximise conception after mating.

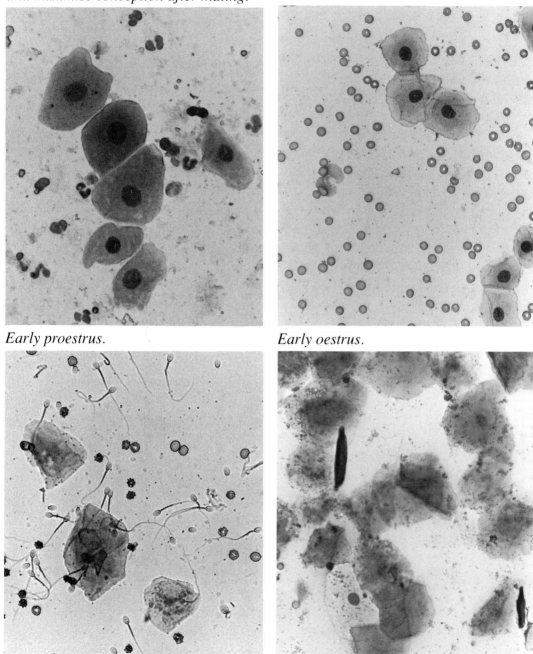

Early proestrus.

Early oestrus.

Mid-oestrus and sperm.

Late oestrus.

bit, but still the vibrator did not work. However, Cartwright had discovered the cause of the problem. With a shout of "Keep the bull there," he flung the switch, with dramatic results, from zero to full power. The bull, with a great bellow, thrust forward, frothed at the mouth, pushed the teaser cow against the wall and evacuated its bowels copiously. To this day, according to Johnson, there is a silhouette of McKinley on the wall of the cowshed, in which a bull received the jolt of his life when trying to mate a cow!

Guide Dogs is now committed to expanding the A.I. programme, and the clinic at the Breeding Centre has been equipped with new and more sophisticated instruments. All collections and storage are undertaken on site, and the unit is being extended with a member of staff being specially trained in Cytology. All bitches are now subjected to a vaginal smear test to establish the time of ovulation in order to maximise conception after mating. Conception has been achieved with some of the frozen semen, but it is still not as reliable as using raw or unfrozen semen, and so natural matings are still the norm. However, progress is being made all the time, and it is hoped that a totally viable and reliable procedure will become possible. Much of the credit for the development of A.I. at Guide Dogs in recent times must go to Gary England, a young and enthusiastic vet, who has been placed on loan to the Association from the Royal Veterinary College Field Station at Potters Bar, Hertfordshire.

Chapter Eight

PREGNANCY AND WHELPING

After the mating of a bitch, some time will elapse before there are any signs that she may have conceived. However, it is important to ensure that any prospective brood bitch does not carry excess weight because this can affect fertility and cause complications when whelping. Sensible diet and adequate exercise well before the date of mating should overcome any of these problems. Regular exercise is important for any dog, but especially in a brood bitch as good muscle tone aids whelping.

All GDBA brood bitches receive booster vaccinations annually. They are boosted the week following the departure of the litter, which is normally when the puppies are six weeks of age. The vaccination will be against distemper, hepatitis, the two leptospirosis diseases and parvo virus. This gives the bitch continual protection and also enables her to pass on protection to her next offspring at a level which appears not to interfere with their early inoculations. She will be round-wormed just prior to mating, and following the mating she will return to her normal routine.

From about the fifth week after mating, the bitch's feed should be split into two parts, because if she is heavily pregnant she might have some difficulty in digesting one large meal. I generally recommend that this is done by splitting the one main meal, and adding a little extra to each, as it is not always necessary to give large quantities of extra food at this time. Extra food can lead to obesity problems, especially if the bitch fails to whelp, and it should only be given if it is needed – for example, if she is obviously carrying a large litter, or for some reason, she is starting to lose condition. At the time the food is split, the bitch should also be receiving a dessertspoonful of sterilised bonemeal, daily, on one of her feeds, and one halibut liver oil capsule about three times a week. Although the in-whelp bitch will undoubtedly benefit from regular exercise, she should be discouraged from jumping and from running with a pack of dogs, where she could get jostled and bumped. It is worth avoiding places such as play areas and parks frequented by dogs, where she will be tempted to run around with the pack and get over-excited and boisterous. These areas can also be health hazards. It is important to keep a careful check on the bitch's health throughout her pregnancy. Any changes in her attitude, especially her feeding and drinking habits, should be noted, as should any abnormal discharges or excessive urination. At GDBA we expect this to be reported to the Breeding Centre, but private breeders should consult their veterinary surgeon. When the bitch is close to whelping, she may need to relieve herself more frequently, and sometimes during the night as well, due to increasing pressure on the kidneys and bladder.

The gestation period is normally nine weeks, or sixty-three days, but it is quite normal for a bitch to be early or a little late. She can safely go over her whelping date by about two or three days, provided she is not showing any signs of distress, and she is generally eating, resting and sleeping in a normal manner, and has a normal temperature (101.3F). The vet needs to be alerted if she has an abnormal discharge, or if she is experiencing contractions that are getting nowhere. Prior to any whelping, an owner should gather together the following equipment and materials:

An ample supply of clean newspaper for bedding.
Clean towels for drying the puppies (and, of course, the bitch).
A suitable box for the puppies while whelping is in progress, especially if the bitch tends to be a little clumsy.
Scales for weighing the puppies and a notebook and pen for recording details of the birth: sex, weight, colour, any abnormalities, and time.
A thermometer for taking the temperature of the bitch.

Surgical gloves.

Round-nose surgical scissors.

Warm water.

Antiseptic lotion for washing down the bitch before and after the whelping.

A sponge.

Drinking bowl.

Milk mixed with glucose for the bitch to drink.

Strong sterilised silk or cotton thread in case a puppy's cord requires tying up.

The milk and glucose should be offered approximately every two hours during the whelping. No solid foods should be given to the bitch until she has completed the whelping cycle, in case there is a sudden and unexpected need for anaesthetic. This can arise, for example, if the bitch needs a caesarian section. I would also recommend that you keep the vet's telephone number handy (for 24-hour cover), should an emergency arise, because it is at these times that the mind goes blank. It is a good idea to notify your vet prior to whelping if you feel that the bitch may have problems, or if you are a little unhappy in your own mind. Most bitches require peace and quiet when they whelp, as they do when mating. A calm owner is far more comfort to an uneasy bitch than an agitated, fussing, overbearing owner, who will only succeed in making matters worse. In fact, a bitch will delay her whelping if she is being interfered with too much, and most do not enjoy an audience. It is sensible to introduce the bitch to the whelping room a week to ten days before she is due, so that she has ample time to settle down and become accustomed to her surroundings.

The bitch should be given plenty of newspapers for bedding, just prior to whelping, and she will then proceed to tear them up to make nests. This activity is, in fact, often the first stage of whelping. The signs of imminent whelping are the bitch scratching the bed and tearing the bedding, rapid panting, and shivering (this is the first stage, accompanied by a drop in her temperature from about 101F to 98F). Sometimes she will start whining or crying. These signs can last for just an hour before whelping commences, or she may continue in this state for as long as twenty-four hours, though her activity will be interrupted with periods of rest. If, however, she shows every sign of whelping throughout this time without relaxing, there is likely to be a problem and your vet should be called. Some bitches refuse food just prior to whelping, but many do not. I have known some Labradors to eat voraciously even if whelping is imminent.

When it is obvious that the bitch is going to whelp, the area that she is in should be raised to a temperature of at least 70F to reduce the possibility of the puppies becoming chilled at birth. Usually the symptoms just described are followed by the start of contractions to expel the foetus (second stage), and the waters will break just prior to a puppy being born. You should ensure that someone is available to attend the bitch while she is actually whelping. When the puppy arrives, check that it is complete and breathing correctly. It should also be checked for any abnormalities such as a cleft palate or hair lip. If its eyes are slightly open it will invariably grow up to be blind and should be put down as soon as possible. In the event of a puppy not breathing, it will be necessary for you to 'swing' it, in order to help the puppy get rid of the fluid which is preventing it from breathing. To do this, clasp both hands securely round the puppy, making sure that its front legs are enclosed within your hands and that the puppy is facing downwards towards the floor. Place both your thumbs firmly on the nape of the puppy's neck to support it, with the index fingers wrapped neatly around the chin to stop the head swinging. Then check there is no wall or obstacle immediately behind you for the puppy to collide with. Place your legs about 18 inches apart and, with a vigorous downward movement, swing the puppy down through your legs, keeping your arms stiff. Do this five or six times until fluid is no longer produced, then rub the puppy well with a rough towel until it is dry and put it back with the bitch. Make sure you massage the pup over a table, and when you are swinging the pup, make sure you are standing over the whelping bed so that if it struggles and slips from your hands, the distance of its fall will be limited and it will land on a soft surface.

If the puppy arrives and the bitch makes no effort to clean or stimulate it, the caul or sac should be broken near the puppy's mouth so that it can breathe. The puppy should then be lifted, plus the after-birth if necessary, and presented to the dam to encourage her to chew and separate the umbilical cord, taking care she does not pull or chew too close to the abdomen. Between a half to one inch of cord should be left to dry and drop off. If she refuses to chew the cord, care should be taken to separate it. Hold the cord firmly, about one and a half inches from the puppy's abdomen, squeezing it tight between finger and thumb, then pull it away from the placenta. Make sure you do not pull the puppy's abdomen. Alternatively, if the bitch is unwilling to chew the cord, use the sterile cotton which you have handy. Tie off the cord at about an inch from the abdomen and cut it off with sterile surgical scissors at about one and a half inches from the abdomen, beyond the tied cotton. The same procedure should apply if there is any haemorrhaging from the cord, even if the bitch has dealt with this naturally. Under no circumstances should the cord be cut with scissors, unless it has been tied previously with sterilised cotton.

Some puppies are born very quickly, some take quite a long time; younger bitches are inclined to whelp more quickly than the older ones. An inexperienced owner

Derek's daughter Helen demonstrates how to swing a puppy in order to release ingested fluid.

may worry because intervals of delivery are not absolutely regular. The bitch may have had four puppies at very regular intervals, and then all of a sudden there is a long delay. The best advice I can give is that if an hour has elapsed, and the bitch is showing signs of contractions and no water has broken, you should scrub up – remove rings, if you wear any – and use the surgical gloves and do an internal investigation with your middle finger. The correct procedure is to lay the bitch flat on her side, get her relaxed and have someone hold her head and reassure her before any investigation is made. Once the bitch is relaxed, investigate carefully to see if you can feel any sign of a foetus blocking the vagina. If not, then the likelihood is that the bitch is resting and that another puppy is on its way, but is not yet ready to be presented. In this case, there is no need to worry. However, if on investigation you can feel an obstruction, either in the form of the head, the back, or even the tail and back legs of a puppy, further action is required. Usually the action of the finger inside the vagina during such an investigation will cause a contraction.

If the investigation reveals that the puppy's back is laid against the aperture, then a veterinary surgeon is required. If, however, it is the pup's nose and head, and it is in the right position, it may well be prudent to wait a little longer. In most cases the puppy will be born satisfactorily. If one of its forelegs is bent back, the leg should be manipulated in line with the head under the chin, so that the bitch can pass the puppy. If this cannot be done, veterinary attention is required. I have found that a puppy the wrong way round, with the back legs coming out, is much easier to deal with. Any pulling should be done very carefully and in rhythm with the bitch's contractions. In the case of a puppy with its hind legs and tail coming first, I often find it easy to trap the tail between my middle and index fingers. I also try to get hold of a back foot as well. Then in rhythm with the contractions of the bitch, and with an assistant applying slight downward pressure on the bitch's abdomen, you can often help the bitch to produce the puppy. The ideal position of the bitch under these circumstances is on her side with her back slightly arched against the wall. The puppy will then be delivered in a slight curve from under the bitch's tail, and not straight out under it.

Most of the books I have read imply that the puppy will be born head and forefeet first, but my experience with thousands of puppies does not support that view. I have seen just as many puppies born hind feet first. It is when puppies are born with legs that are not following through, hind feet first with legs trapped back, head folded back or completely breeched and laid across the entrance with a back presentation that the real problems occur. Under these circumstances surgical intervention is usually needed to relieve the situation, and a vet should be called immediately.

Sometimes a long wait can be followed by the birth of a dead puppy. This can have been holding up the delivery of the remaining members of the litter, who will then come forward rather more quickly. It is not unusual to find a dead puppy in a litter, and generally there is no reason to be concerned about it. Something will have gone wrong with that particular foetus, and normally there is no need to worry about the other puppies still to be born. There is no pattern to where dead puppies arrive in the litter. However, there does seem to be one factor which shows up from time to time. If an older bitch produces a mammoth puppy that is dead, it invariably signals the end of her breeding life. Needless to say, any dead puppy should be removed immediately from the bitch so that she does not grieve for it or become anxious about it. Encourage her to concentrate on caring for the living ones and to get on with the whelping.

It is not easy to determine when the bitch has finished whelping. The only sure test, of course, is an X-ray, but you can usually tell when it is over because the bitch will become relaxed and want to settle down to sleep. However, this can happen if she is having a rest between delivery of puppies. The procedure I adopt, once the bitch has had a number of puppies and decides to settle down, is to check by palpation of the abdomen whether there are further puppies. I lie the bitch on her side on the flat surface of her bed, having removed all the bedding. The left hand is

Brood bitch 'Tessa' and family in an indoor whelping kennel designed by Derek.

placed under her abdomen with the back of the hand flat on the bed, the palm facing upward. The right hand is then used to feel her tummy. Try to feel the left hand, which is placed on the bed, but if you encounter round, tubular objects with either hand you can assume there is a further pup to be whelped. It might also be a retained after-birth. If it is a puppy, you should be able to detect a hard bony part to the tubular object, which is the puppy's head. If you cannot detect anything hard, the chances are that any object will be an after-birth. and you can safely bed the bitch down and retire yourself, leaving her to nurse her litter. However, you need to check again the next day to see if the object has disappeared during the night, for she may well have passed and eaten the after-birth. Check her temperature regularly for the three days after whelping. A sudden rise may indicate a retained after-birth or a puppy, in which case you should immediately contact the vet. A sonic scanner, which we have recently acquired, detects the sound of the puppy's heartbeat, but of course, it will not tell you if there is still a dead puppy in there. The attitude, temperature and general health of the bitch during whelping and for the three days after, are still all-important factors. If a bitch is taking a long time to whelp and you know there are still puppies to come and are concerned that her contractions may be weakening, contact your vet and get him to come and give her an oxytocine injection which promotes fuller, stronger contractions. It can also, I believe, help to stimulate milk production.

If the abdomen appears to be clear and the bitch is indicating that she wants to get down to rest, feed her a good light diet of something like glucose and milk, or gruel or gravy; bed her down and leave her. The chances are that she has finished whelping, but do not be too surprised if you get up the next morning to find that in spite of all your investigations there are eight instead of seven puppies. During a prolonged whelping you must allow the bitch to leave the nest. She may need encouragement to go out and relieve herself, as she may be protective about her newborn puppies. The best way to encourage her is to pick up one of pups and let her see you moving with it out of the kennel. This invariably does the trick, particularly if the pup is making noises. Slip on the leash and do not allow her to go into the garden or run alone while she is relieving herself – she could well drop a valuable puppy. I have experienced this on numerous occasions. In order to save the puppy having a concrete landing at night, take a torch with you. During whelping the bitch should be offered milk and glucose at about two-hourly intervals or, if this is not available, some other liquid such as stock, broth or egg and milk. If there is any kind of problem with either the bitch or the whelps, contact the vet. If in doubt, don't mess about: seek expert advice.

After whelping you should wash and dry the bitch. The main areas to wash are directly underneath the tail and down the feathering of the hind legs, as she could develop skin problems from amniotic fluid. Any mild liquid soap can be used, mixed with warm water and applied liberally with a sponge. Then bed her down with her puppies. She should be given plenty of soft bedding such as newspapers, shredded paper without print is better, or, if you are particularly affluent, wood wool. Clean paper (e.g. sanitary packaging paper) is excellent: it is economical, easy to use, and hygienic. Its thermal properties are ideal for puppies and, unlike wood wool or straw, it lasts well and does not quickly break down into dust. I do not, following bitter experience, recommend hay or straw as bedding. Both can harbour parasites and promote skin and respiratory troubles in puppies. During and immediately after whelping, the bedding can become extremely wet and messy and needs to be changed regularly. If possible, burn the old bedding.

Before moving on to the care of the brood and her puppies, let me touch on one other subject: the use of heat lamps during whelping and afterwards. At GDBA we have tried various types and have finally settled for a 250-watt dull emitter. I have found them to be very beneficial, but there is a danger if the lamp is hung too low over the whelping bitch, particularly if she is not able to move away from the direct heat. A caring dam will frequently lie there and suffer, staying with her litter rather than abandoning them. We have a minimum height for the lamp, which is marked with a clear red stripe on the wall immediately at the back of the lamp. Any member of staff dealing with a litter can immediately see if the lamp is too low. In addition, the chain from which the lamp is hung is only long enough for it to reach the safety level. The length of chain and the position of the red tape will depend upon the size of the individual brood bitch – the larger the dog, the higher the lamp from the bed. In order to assess where the red line should be, we place cardboard boxes in the nest area, set up the lamp and put the maximum-minimum thermometer on top of the boxes at a height that corresponds with a bitch's head when she is lying down. The temperature should never register above 85F; otherwise the bitch might become dehydrated or suffer from heat stroke.

One night many years ago, before we took adequate precautions, I arrived back at our Breeding Centre after a long journey to find a very distressed brood bitch with a day-old litter. She had a temperature of 105F and was panting and looked extremely distressed. I watched for a short while to see what was happening, but I could not find anything wrong, despite the signs of distress. She continued to pant heavily and would not settle with her puppies, although it was approaching midnight. I immediately rang our vet and although he was in bed he agreed to come out to see what was amiss, possibly fearing some kind of virus infection which would require his attention. While I was waiting for him, I attempted to calm the bitch down and then I realised that the lamp in the kennel was far too low over her and the litter. Her instinct had told her to stay with her pups and, as a result, she had become dehydrated, although the pups were comfortable. Once I realised this, I immediately put her in a bath of fairly cold water, which brought her temperature down to a reasonable level. This was what the vet found when he arrived a few minutes later. He confirmed that the lamp height was to blame, and after we raised it there were no more problems with the bitch and her litter. This naturally led me to realise that we must have some safeguard against a similar situation occurring again. We also place a rubber mat on the floor where the bitch can go if she wants to be away from the direct beam of the lamp. We eventually get the bitch to use the 'sanctuary', which are all wall-mounted, and she can survey her family while resting.

Chapter Nine

THE NURSING BITCH AND HER PUPPIES

The bitch must be allowed some privacy for the first few days after whelping to enable her to settle with the puppies. She should not, under any circumstances, be subjected to a continual stream of visitors looking at her and handling her puppies. Many bitches, and not necessarily only first-timers, can be quite disturbed for the first two days. It is common for a bitch to refuse the opportunity to go and relieve herself because she wants to stay with her puppies. Again, the best remedy is to take a puppy out in your hand and the bitch will follow you to the relief area. Do be careful with the more frantic bitch when she goes back into the whelping box. I have seen one bitch accidentally nick off a puppy's ear in her desire to get back quickly amongst her babies. In this situation you need to steady her down and ensure that there are no visitors beside the bed when she returns. An anxious state of mind does not tend to last too long, but it is very important that you exercise sympathetic control during those first few days until she is settled and becomes confident.

Having a crowd around her whelping box is a certain way of unsettling the bitch, and it has been known for the bitch to savage her pups or even abandon them completely because of constant interruptions from people other than the immediate family known to her. This applies particularly to a bitch with her first litter.

Visitors should only be allowed to see the puppies after their first week when the bitch has become more relaxed, and they should remain unobtrusive and as far away as possible, preferably looking through a window to avoid the risk of any infection. Do not forget that humans as well as dogs can carry infection into whelping areas, and visitors should never be allowed to handle the puppies. Owners should also take care that they do not pass on disease through contact with other dogs. On the whole, I prefer visitors to keep away until the puppies are at least four weeks old, and even then there should be restrictions.

It is quite normal for the bitch to have a slight discharge from the vulva for anything up to two months after the whelping, and providing it is not excessive or particularly offensive, there is nothing to worry about. It is also normal for the bitch's faeces to be loose and dark in colour; they can often be black, through cleaning up, for a few days after whelping. This should return to normal within about a week.

The puppies' claws need to be checked weekly and clipped, if necessary, to prevent them from injuring the bitch when they suckle. As an alternative to clipping with scissors, you can use a nail file or patent nail clippers. In GDBA the front and hind dew claws are removed. There is no necessity to remove the front ones, which are used to good effect by dogs who chew bones, but guide dog owners prefer it. It is better if hind dew claws, are removed, although this may depend upon the breed requirements, as some breed standards require that they are retained. Normally they are removed by a qualified vet between the third and sixth day after birth, depending on how well the puppy is doing.

Ideally the puppies should almost double their birth weight within the first week and maintain a steady increase in weight over the next five to six weeks. It is, therefore, important to weigh the puppies when they are born and at regular intervals thereafter. An interesting exercise is to keep a graph of each puppy's weight taken at weekly intervals. The males will usually progress faster than the females.

While the bitch is nursing her litter, her exercise should be restricted to the house and garden. She must never be taken for walks down the road or allowed to free-run in parks. This, again, is to ensure that there is the minimum risk of infection being brought back to the nest. The same precaution should apply to any other dog living in the house with the bitch and puppies. If a GDBA puppy is the second dog, we try to arrange for it to be temporarily puppy-walked in another home so that its education is not interrupted through having to have its walks curtailed. I learnt with my first German Shepherd bitch of the high risk of transfer of disease. She had whelped a very nice litter and they were thriving. The pups had reached about four weeks of age, when I visited an aunt who lived at the opposite side of the valley. I felt quite safe visiting her because she had never owned dogs, and I realised even then that it was risky to go among other dogs. However, during the course of my visit my aunt asked if I would look at her daughter's dog that was staying in the house. It was in the kitchen and not feeling very well. A cold shudder went down my back when I asked what was wrong with the dog and was told that it had dirty eyes, a filthy discharge from the nose, and had recently developed a cough. I apologised for refusing to look at the dog, and explained that I had a valuable litter at home that I did not want to infect. I advised them to get a vet as quickly as possible. My fears were confirmed when the following day the dog was put down with distemper. I took the obvious precaution when going home of disinfecting my shoes and not taking them into the kennel area, but I could not do that with my clothing. Within ten days my bitch and her litter had contracted distemper. I lost half the litter, and I almost lost the valuable bitch. It was a very salutary lesson in animal husbandry which I have never forgotten. We ensure that all GDBA brood bitch owners are aware of the care that must be taken with valuable puppies.

If a vet is needed, he must be asked to make a home visit. If your own vet will not turn out and it is an emergency, try to contact another practice. Although this may cost you extra money it is well worth it, as it should only be in exceptional circumstances that a young uninoculated pup, whelping bitch or bitch with whelps should be taken down to a surgery where, of course, there could be numerous sick animals. The only exception to this rule is if the bitch needs a caesarian section, which can only be carried out at the surgery, or if surgery is needed on a puppy – but there is a risk when it returns to the nest. If a visit to the surgery is unavoidable, it is advisable to allow the bitch or puppy to remain in your car until the vet is able to see it. Never, under any circumstances, allow the animal in a waiting room at the surgery – especially a pup that has not yet received any protective injections.

The diet required by a brood bitch varies from one individual to the next, and you must use your judgement rather than follow slavishly the instructions in books, or on the labels of many proprietary dog foods which specify exact quantities for particular breeds and body weights. No bitch that is nursing a full litter should be offered less than three meals a day, as well as an adequate supply of fluid. The amount of each feed will depend on her individual needs. For the first twenty-four hours after whelping, she will require only liquid feeds, and these should take the form of milk, gravy or stock, and should be offered at two-hourly intervals. After this, she should carefully be brought back on to a normal diet. I suggest you offer such things as eggs, scrambled or boiled, lightly cooked meat, and biscuits or brown bread soaked in gravy or stock. It is important to continue giving a calcium supplement in the form of bonemeal, raw bone or Calocal D to the bitch for about three to four weeks after the puppies have left her. This helps her to rebuild any deficiency that might have occurred. About forty-eight hours after whelping, the bitch can be gently brought back on to raw meat and dry biscuit. The following diet sheet is the one we recommend for all GDBA broods and litters:

7. 00am: Milk and glucose, or milk and cereal.
9.00am: Meat and biscuit, brown bread soaked in milk or stock, if required.
11.30am: Milk and glucose or milk and cereal (approx one to one and a half pints).
2.00pm: Meat and biscuit, brown bread soaked in milk or stock, if required.
4.00pm: Milk and glucose.
8.00pm: Meat and biscuit, brown bread soaked in milk or stock, if required.

Bonemeal should be added to one meat feed at the rate of about one dessertspoon daily. One halibut or cod liver oil capsule should be given twice or three times a week (medium/large breed dogs). Sheep's heads or breasts of mutton can be offered as an alternative to the usual meat. Gravy or stock also can be substituted for milk, if this is preferred, now that the bitch has whelped. Clean water must be available at all times, but special care must be taken that the puppies cannot accidentally reach it, or they could drown. When the puppies are between ten days and three weeks of age, according to the litter size and progress, you can start to wean them. Normally, I believe in early weaning, but there are some litters, particularly where the bitch enjoys having her puppies with her and the pups are progressing well, that can be left for longer than the sixteen days or so, which is our normal guide.

The procedure in most of the breeding kennels I have known is to introduce the puppies to a liquid diet, getting them to lap milk first. This is not generally our approach. We find it much easier to get the puppy to suck your fingers covered with scraped raw lean meat, or one of the top-quality canned meats, without lumps. Once we get the puppy enjoying the taste of the meat from the finger, it graduates to taking it from the dish. At first, the food is taken from the security of the kennel girl's lap, who talks to and handles the puppy, thus socialising it at the same time. Pups then move on to soaked puppy biscuit and finely-minced meat, preferably raw with minimal fat. This is alternated with a milk cereal feed, preferably Weetabix which, in our experience, is one of the better products for young stock. We have also tried certain proprietary weaning foods, with success. It is important to check that this food does not stick to the roof of the puppy's mouth. It was a problem with one

Weaning usually starts when the puppies are around sixteen days old.

particular product, but with care it is has nevertheless proved excellent for getting young puppies going. Mix the feed and allow it to stand for a time before feeding, to allow any expansion to occur. Then liquidise again just prior to offering it to the puppies.

To begin with, one teaspoon of scraped raw beef for each puppy twice a day is sufficient, feeding it from the back of a teaspoon or the finger. After a few more days, start to introduce milky cereal feeds, giving the milk in a shallow dish. Each puppy will vary in the amount it is able to take at one time, and therefore care should be taken not to force too much into it. Each day a little more meat should be added, gradually increasing the size of the feeds as the puppies grow. Soaked biscuit (or soaked brown bread) can be added to the meat feed, but never white bread. Watch for any shy feeders, and spend a little extra time encouraging them. It is very easy for these pups to be pushed out by the more dominant members of the litter, and if that happens they could well fall behind.

Some breeders and vets frown at cow's milk, but GDBA brood bitch owners have fed many, many litters on it, very successfully. I do have some reservations about proprietary powdered milk. We have used quite a number of brands over the years

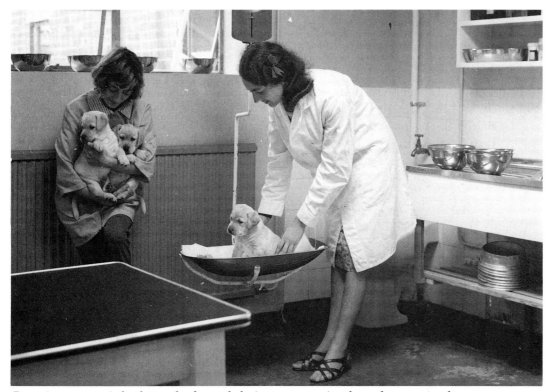

Puppies are weighed regularly and their progress is plotted on a graph.

and, as many of them seem to give the puppies loose motions, we eventually settled for Roberts Weaning Food, with excellent results. Brown bread has very good value in puppy-weaning, particularly when it is soaked in stock, gravy or broth made from sheep's heads. If you have a source, goat's milk is an excellent product. We have used it successfully for many years when we had members of staff who owned goats and were able to ensure a good supply. Most of it was frozen: remember that any form of puppy diet must not be fed chilled, i.e. straight from the fridge. Ideally, it should be slightly warmed up, so that there is no chill to the puppy's tummy.

If puppies are not fed properly at this stage of their development, they can develop bent legs or rickets, and some will fail to thrive. Many puppies have internal parasites, especially Toxocara canis (roundworm). If they are not receiving nourishing food and are harbouring a bad worm infestation, they will finish up as very emaciated pups, which could set them back for the rest of their lives. Keen observation is essential, and any problems should be dealt with at a very early age. The progress of every puppy in a litter should be monitored and recorded. Litters will thrive at different rates, but ideally, the males and females should be making a steady climb that will show on a graph. At GDBA we maintain these graphs until the litter is about six weeks of age, when the puppies are placed in the puppy walker's home. At this point they should not show any signs of overweight, nor should they be thin or emaciated. They should have good bone structure and strength, and be well covered with flesh. Thin or weedy pups, bloated pot-bellied pups and overweight pups usually finish up with problems, and it is important to aim at rearing a well-balanced litter of healthy vigorous puppies, all of whom have a healthy appetite and are not susceptible to disease through poor nourishment.

Once the puppies are weaned, which should be by the time they are five to six weeks old, they should be following the diet sheet below. Times can be altered to suit household routines:

8.00 am: Milk and cereal feed or weaning food (Roberts Laughing Dog).
11.00 am: Meat and puppy biscuit (or soaked brown bread).
2.00 pm: Milk or gravy (or stock).
5.00 pm: Meat and puppy biscuit (or soaked brown bread).
8.00 pm: Milk and cereal or weaning food.
Bonemeal should be added to one feed only, at the rate of one teaspoon daily. All puppies should receive one halibut liver oil capsule, no more than twice weekly.

As the puppies are weaned, the bitch's diet should be adjusted to help her to dry off. Milk and other fluids should be restricted, and protein, which makes milk, should be reduced. Her diet should be decreased gradually, so that when the puppies are completely weaned she should almost be back to her normal intake of food. This procedure will help to dry off her milk and so make her feel more comfortable. With GDBA, once the puppies have been collected for puppy walking, the bitch's normal exercise can be resumed, which will help to reduce the milk-flow. In my opinion, no further vitamin or supplement should be required by the majority of bitches. If she is a good milk producer and is rather slow in drying up, place a small amount of Epsom salts, enough to cover your middle finger nail, on the back of the bitch's tongue night and morning. Alternatively, you can get milk suppressant tablets from your vet.

A number of conditions may arise at the time of whelping, or just after, which call for some comment:

MASTITIS: This is a hardening of one or more of the mammary glands on the bitch, and is usually accompanied by a rise in temperature. The affected gland, or

Labrador puppies at four weeks, still enjoy the security of their mother's presence.

glands, will be hot, hard and extremely painful, and there is an understandable reluctance on the bitch's part to feed her puppies. The normal procedure in this case is to contact the vet as quickly as possible and he will usually prescribe an antibiotic. However, I do have some reservations about this, as there have been some occasions in my experience, where the mastitis has been fairly advanced and the pus has set hard, and antibiotics have not relieved the situation. You are then left with two options: the condition can be alleviated by surgery, or you can apply very hot fermentations, consisting of T.C.P. and water, or Epsom salts and water, with a cloth, which should be wrung out to become as dry as possible to avoid scalding. These should be applied every two hours for ten to fifteen minutes. Try to draw the milk away from the affected glands, and then massage. In some cases the puppies may have to be hand-reared, or weaned earlier than usual. I have personally applied this method on many occasions with great success.

ECLAMPSIA: Eclampsia is the result of a massive and very sudden calcium deficiency. The symptoms are fluctuating temperature, which goes from normal to sub-normal, accompanied by rapid panting, shivering, unsteady gait, glazed eyes and convulsions. The nursing bitch with this condition requires veterinary attention immediately, as death follows the onset of symptoms within hours if it is untreated. Eclampsia is inclined to occur mainly between the second and third weeks of lactation, and although bitches with large litters seem to be most prone, it can affect any lactating bitch. It is not a particularly common condition, but when it does occur it is very serious. The calcium she is lacking cannot be given in tablet or medicine form; it must either be injected into the bitch or given by drip. I have only seen three or four cases of eclampsia in my time with GDBA, and I wouldn't blame them on incorrect feeding. The animals continued as brood bitches, and all reared litters with no recurrence of the problem. However, a product known as Calo-calc-D was given as a daily additive to their diet as a precaution from the first day of gestation.

RETAINED PLACENTA (AFTERBIRTH) OR PUPPY: This is indicated by a sudden rise in temperature, up to 103F or more, accompanied by shivers, rapid panting, sometimes an offensive-smelling vaginal discharge and a loss of appetite. Veterinary attention is essential.

WORMING PROGRAMME

Worming should be started when the puppies are four weeks of age to get rid of roundworms (Toxocara canis). Worming products can be obtained from your vet or from a good chemist, and each puppy should be dosed according to its weight and the instructions. After dosing, a careful check should be kept on each puppy and the results should be recorded. The faeces of each puppy need to be checked, a tedious task, but essential for good animal husbandry. The dose should be repeated every ten days until at least two negative results are obtained, and if one or two puppies pass worms, it is best to assume that the whole litter is affected. The tablets will only eliminate adult worms and will not affect the larvae which are migrating within the puppy. It will not destroy the eggs, which will eventually hatch out, migrate and become worms within ten days. Hence the need for two consecutive negative returns, with a ten day interval between worming.

The faeces should be examined for evidence of worms, but this can only serve as a rough guide; if there is any doubt, faeces samples should be taken to the vet and examined under a microscope. There are many proprietary brands of worm tablets on the market, and not all are totally effective. Therefore it is dangerous to assume that a worm infestation has been cleared by giving the puppy just one treatment. I would suggest you ask other breeders or a vet which brand they recommend, because new and more effective remedies are continually being put on the market. The most effective routine is to continue worming the puppies periodically for the first six months of life and to check samples under a microscope.

After the the puppies have departed for their new homes, the brood bitch should be wormed, again until two consecutive negative results have been obtained at ten day intervals. Roundworms look like lengths of very thin, wiry string, usually pinkish in colour. Tapeworms, which rarely seem to be found in puppies under five months of age, are long, flat worms which tend to be whiter in colour. They are a lot flatter than the roundworms and appear in segments, which are shorter than the roundworm. When seen in the faeces they can be compared to grains of rice, or small sections of flat tape.

Tapeworms frequently adhere to the hindquarters and the feathering. Their life cycle is not within the dog, for in order to survive they need an intermediary host such as sheep, rabbits or fleas. The eggs are contained in the tail segment of the worm and are passed out of the dog in its faeces; they can be found stuck to the hair under the tail. These segments contain millions of eggs. The eggs are eventually eaten by the host, where they develop into cysts and lodge in the brain. They remain dormant until eaten again, this time by the dog, when they develop into an adult worm. This brief description of the tapeworm's life-cycle shows how necessary it is to cook sheep's brain or rabbit offal before they are fed to a dog, and the importance of checking that the bitch and her puppies are free from fleas. If you suspect that the bitch has a tapeworm and she is carrying or nursing puppies, it is advisable to leave the worming treatment until the puppies are fully weaned. If the presence of worms is affecting her condition, veterinary advice is advisable. The bitch will not pass tapeworms directly to her puppies, but worming her during lactation could have a bad effect on her puppies.

There are a number of other problems which may affect a brood and her new pups. The bitch may be reluctant, or refuse to feed her puppies – she may even refuse to stay with them. More often than not, there is no obvious physical problem with the bitch such as a swollen abdomen, mastitis or soreness caused by the puppies scratching. It could be that the bitch is being constantly disturbed by people looking at her puppies. It is also worth checking that the heat lamp, if one is in use, is not too low over her bed. Make sure that the bitch has enough food and fluid to produce milk. A medium to large sized bitch with a full litter should be given at least three pints of milk or stock daily. Fresh water should be available to her at all times. If the puppies are crying and appear unsettled, check to see if there are any physical problems with them. The bitch may be experiencing symptoms of a retained placenta or of dead puppies that have not been born. Have a close look at her teats. If they are blocked, a gentle massage should get them back into full operation. Make sure that she is receiving enough protein to meet her lactation demands. Raw meat is the best form of protein, and her intake of this may well have to be stepped up to improve her milk supply. I recall the case of one very good brood who initially had difficulty feeding her litter and lost weight dramatically until we tripled her meat supply, after which there was a big improvement in the amount and quality of her milk.

A very distressing condition is when puppies fail to thrive. If this occurs, first check for any physical abnormality in the affected puppies for example, cleft palate, hare lip or even constipation. Very small, weak puppies need to have their living temperature raised above 80F. In order to achieve this, you may need to move the puppies into an incubator and just return them to the bitch at regular intervals to feed. Try to avoid fluctuations in temperature, as this may cause the puppies to chill. At GDBA we are fortunate enough to have an incubator on hand which has been specifically designed for this task. However, a proprietary brand of electrical plant propagator with a thermostat, costing a few pounds, is more than adequate for the job, and we have many brood bitch holders who have used them successfully. The subject of failing puppies is extremely complex, and I would not pretend to understand all the causes. However, a number of years back we carried out an investigation in conjunction with a survey conducted by Tony Blythe, who then was working at the Animal Health Trust. Our figures showed that the proportion of

GDBA puppies that faded within forty-eight hours was only eight to nine per cent, whereas the average in the country as a whole appeared to be nearer thirty per cent. The only reason we could think of for the disparity was the strict hygiene code that we observe with all our bitches and puppies. Since that survey, there has been no significant change in the figures either way, although our number of broods and subsequent whelpings has dramatically increased.

In the case of puppies who appear reluctant to feed, as well as those who may be fading, remove the puppies from the bitch and place them in an incubator. They must be given nourishment every two hours, and ideally, they should be allowed to suckle the bitch or foster mother from one of the better teats – one that has a good shape and shows evidence of a good milk flow. Press the pup's mouth around the teat and hold it up against the bitch's udder, at the same time pressing the puppy gently from behind so that he is close into the bitch – this will assist the milk flow. Another trick is to use the index finger on your free hand to gently massage the tip of the puppy's nose, which will encourage it to suckle. If this fails, draw milk into a 2cc syringe, or a Belcroy Feeder, and physically hand-rear the puppy for a time.

It is also well worth checking to see if the puppy can suck. Moisten your little finger with the bitch's milk and place it in the puppy's mouth. If it is sucking well you will feel it. Check that the bitch has milk, and watch that the milk is not returning down the puppy's nose, which is a bad sign. Place your ear close to the rib cage and listen to its breathing for signs of fluid on the lungs. In the event of the bitch's milk being unacceptable to the puppy and no foster-mother being available, a product known as Whelpi can be used. We have used it with excellent results.

It is natural for a bitch, particularly one with a strong maternal instinct, to regurgitate her food for her puppies. She does it to wean them and the puppies stimulate her by nuzzling and licking her lips. The owner may find it objectionable, but no harm can come from it, providing that no hard bone has been fed to the bitch and she has not been under any form of medication which may be passed through her mouth to the puppies. It is quite a difficult habit to overcome and there is really no need to try, although keeping her away from the litter for a while after a meal may help. Do not be surprised or concerned when you see the bitch clear up and swallow the faeces and urine produced by her puppies. It is quite normal. She is merely keeping the nest clean and should be allowed and encouraged to do so; yet it is surprising the number of queries I have had about this habit from people who are rearing a litter for the first time. Some puppies may require stimulation to urinate and defecate, and occasionally the bitch is reluctant, or even unable to help, particularly after surgery. In this instance, you will need to gently massage the pup's genitals and rectum with a wad of moist cotton wool to produce a response.

Occasionally, puppies are born as 'swimmers'. These are slow to stand up. Their front and hind legs are usually spread out from their bodies, and they seem unable to take the pup's weight. In fact, they move by 'swimming' along on their chests and stomachs, hence the name. Often, on examination, the rib cage is found to be quite flat between the front legs – a condition that can be detected as early as three weeks of age. Should any of our brood bitch owners see this in a litter, we ask them to report it immediately to the Breeding Centre, as remedial treatment needs to be undertaken. The first thing we would check is the weight of the puppy. A number that I have seen have been overweight, which makes it more difficult for them to get on their feet. In these cases, it is necessary to gradually reduce the time that the puppy spends feeding, thus reducing its intake of food. Swimmers often appear in small litters where individuals do not have to fight for a place on the milk bar, and therefore do not need to move very much. These puppies should be encouraged to move around more in the nest, and they should also be taken out of the nest wherever possible to be given individual exercise.

One method I have tried, with success, is to place a plank a few inches from a wall and then encourage the puppy to walk up and down within this artificial channel. The width of the channel is such that the puppy's legs cannot splay out. Repeat the exercise five or six times a day for a period of five or ten minutes each time. Another device, which was actually patented by one of our brood bitch holders, is a canvas sling which allows the puppy to be suspended for a short time with its four legs hanging down. A less obvious idea is to put the puppy at about three or four weeks old in a shallow tub of lukewarm water and allow it to swim. Again, this needs to be done four or five times a day for five or ten minutes at a time. I have found this to be one of the best exercises for getting a swimmer pup up on to its feet. Some years ago swimmers were always put down. I have seen half a dozen or so in GDBA, and where I have persisted with one or more of the methods described, the puppies have survived and gone on to become vigorous and healthy adult dogs. One, in fact, became a brood bitch. She went on to produce five litters, totalling thirty-six puppies, and before she died in September 1974, eight-six per cent of her progeny had become guide dogs. None of the unsuccessful offspring had the same problem.

Chapter Ten

THE CAMPAIGN FOR EARLY INOCULATION

When I arrived at Guide Dogs in 1959, the inoculation procedure was to give all stock an injection of serum as soon as it arrived. At that time there were two brands available, both of which were supposed to give immediate protection against distemper and hardpad. Their effect receded quickly, and after three weeks the protection level was thought to have dropped to almost zero. The adult stock coming into kennels were given a testing period of three weeks, at the end of which a decision had to be made whether one was going to keep them for training or send them home. If their previous owners did not want them back, we would find suitable pet homes. Those that were kept were then given vaccine, normally Burroughs Wellcome Epivax, which protected against hardpad, distemper and hepatitis, and Leptovax against leptospirosis, canicola and icterohaemorrhagiae. A fortnight later a booster of Leptovax was given. If a dog was being sent back to its owner, we tended not to give it a vaccine; but rejects which were going to completely new owners were vaccinated. Of course, we tried to get dogs in that had already been inoculated, in order to ensure that they were protected, and to save money.

Young puppies were also given a serum injection before being placed in a puppy walker's home. In those days the average age at which we would place a puppy would be between ten and twelve weeks. We even accepted and placed puppies at sixteen weeks, which we would never do now. In spite of giving serum, a great number of pups, within a day or two of placing, and even before going out, suffered from sickness and diarrhoea. Many had the symptoms of distemper, with dirty eyes and runny noses and a high temperature. When checked, many had active distemper infection, and the puppy either died or lost condition and fell behind in physical and temperamental qualities. In some cases the nervous system would also be damaged and fits developed, and we probably finished up with a reject. We would invariably lose the puppy walker as well.

We clearly needed a better procedure, because I was already pushing to get puppies out at an earlier age. I had a strong belief in Scott Fuller's work in America, which showed that the earlier you conditioned a puppy to the environment to which it would be exposed as an adult, the better it would survive and perform. This also applied to a companion dog. We therefore contacted Burroughs Wellcome, who advised us to take blood samples from our eight to ten broods when they were five weeks in whelp. Anti-body levels in each sample were then analysed to show when the maternal immunity would have receded. We looked at the titre counts of our brood stock over a period of time, and we found that the majority had low titre levels, which indicated that their litters could then be protected with vaccine at the very early age of six weeks. The only two exceptions, curiously enough, were some Malemute puppies which we had at the time. Their dam's immunity was very low, possibly because she belonged to one of the last domesticated breeds to enter the UK and had never encountered distemper. As a result, her puppies could have been given the vaccine in the first week of their lives and would have acquired immunity. The mother's immunity was so low that she had to be regularly boosted. A German Shepherd bitch, named Reiner, also had a low antibody count, and it was noticeable that one of her puppies had very low immunity to distemper. It is said that a dog cannot have active distemper twice, as they gain antibodies which give them protection. That particular dog undoubtedly had distemper three times, in spite of also being twice fully vaccinated within the first year of life. Each time we checked the titre counts of the pup and its dam, and they were always very low. Interestingly, this pup was the product of an in-bred mating.

As a result of these titre counts from bitches in whelp, and on the advice of Burroughs Wellcome, we started giving distemper and Leptospirosis vaccine

Puppies receive their first inoculation at six weeks, before going to a puppy walker.

initially to nine week-old puppies, repeating the full dose at twelve weeks. Leptovax was given again at fourteen weeks. We have now been doing early inoculations, at six weeks, for well over twenty-five years, and the policy has paid off. Once we went over to the new procedure, there was an immediate change in the picture. Puppies receiving the vaccine were walked daily, maintained steady progress and few became sick.

The success of the early inoculations helped us to our present policy of early socialisation of puppies, because it quickly became evident that we could get them out even younger than nine weeks. At the time, the standard advice from most vaccine manufacturers was that twelve weeks was the ideal time for inoculations to commence. Earlier immunization, in their view, could occasionally lead to failure of the vaccine, because of a persistent maternal immunity. However, we were prepared to take the risk of an occasional puppy becoming sick in order to gain early exposure for the majority. Despite much criticism from the veterinary profession, we started placing puppies at six weeks of age, after vaccinating them against hardpad, distemper, hepatitis and leptospirosis. We told puppy walkers to get their puppies out, but not to take them to parks where other dogs went: they should not allow the puppy to sniff at lamp-posts and other places marked by dogs, and they should be very selective about mixing with other dogs. In high risk areas, it was sufficient just to carry the pup and let it see life in busy urban areas. In most situations we felt quite happy for the puppy to be put on the floor before it had its full inoculations, which came at twelve weeks of age with another complete set of inoculations against hardpad, distemper, hepatitis and leptospirosis; and at fourteen weeks they had a further leptospirosis jab.

At twelve weeks they would have been out on the puppy scheme for five or six weeks, and the inoculation would be given by the home vet using vaccine from his own stock. Vaccines could be reclaimed from the various manufacturers, with whom we have an agreement for concessionary rates, but most vets were very kind and let us have the vaccines free of charge. The policy did not cause any problems, and although there was a wide variety of vaccines available, the vast majority proved reliable.

The record speaks for itself. I can count on one hand the number of pups we have lost in the last twenty-five years, or more, with either active distemper, hardpad or hepatitis, although some were being walked in areas where distemper infections were rampant. Well over 24,000 puppies have now passed safely through our puppy-walking scheme to become good, sound guide dogs.

In the past, our advice was to give boosters once a year after the dogs had qualified, but this is now left to the discretion of the individual vets, who have their own views on whether full boosters are needed in their particular area, particularly in the case of hepatitis where live vaccine is sometimes used. With this one form of vaccine there was possibly a small danger of keratitis (blue-eye). In fact, I have only seen three cases, and none left any permanent eye damage. The condition seemed to last about two to three weeks before it responded to veterinary treatment. With the Adeno 2 virus used in present-day vaccines the risk of blue-eye has been eliminated.

Our policy of early inoculation resulted in many battles with the veterinary profession. We were often arguing with vets, who followed a policy of advising pet owners not to allow their puppies to see the light of day until they were seventeen weeks old. Obviously, this would have been disastrous for guide dog puppies, where early socialization is vital. In the early days we also had to take on the vaccine manufacturers, and dispute their findings. In the sixties when we introduced an early vaccination policy I recall talking to a representative from a vaccine manufacturer, who advised us to vaccinate early. I asked why his company did not advocate this to the veterinary profession at large. He replied that they were in a competitive market, and other vaccine manufacturers were advocating that one inoculation, given then at nine weeks of age, would give protection for a year, or in some cases, for life. If his company put their product on the market saying it could be given at six weeks, but the pup would require to have a further full course at nine weeks, this would mean that customers would have to pay twice the cost to get the same sort of protection, which was not a good commercial proposition. Many dog owners and vets are still not aware of the temperamental damage which can be caused to a puppy by keeping it in isolation until it is old enough to have completed a course of inoculations. In most cases, the course does not even begin until the puppy is on the deadline regarding the critical socialisation time to be exposed to urban life. The reality and value of Burroughs Wellcome advice on early vaccination was so outstandingly good that the benefits to our dogs were immediately observed.

Today, most manufacturers advise early inoculations, providing that the puppy is re-vaccinated later, so it does seem that most manufacturers now recognise the benefits. However, in the sixties we were pioneering the idea, and we were criticised by veterinary surgeons from all over the country. The majority of vets still advocate starting the inoculation course at twelve weeks, and some advise puppy walkers to isolate their dogs until the course has been completed, even though each puppy has been inoculated at six weeks. This causes confusion and anxiety among our walkers. Our policy is to advise them against getting into a battle with the vet, but to continue taking the puppy out and about. We stress that the puppy has received initial protection. At twelve weeks the vast majority of puppies have been out and about, but on occasions where the walker has still been advised by their vet to keep a puppy in isolation until it has received the second jab at fourteen weeks to protect it from leptospirosis, we have to insist that they take our advice as owners of the puppy.

I have lost count of the number of telephone calls I have received from vets 'advising' me about the risks we were taking with our puppies. I would always refer them to our Centre vets, in order to convince them that we did understand their problem, but perhaps they did not really understand ours. Eventually we placed the GDBA inoculation policy on record in Association literature – and it is in there to this very day – that we, The Guide Dog for the Blind Association, were prepared to take the risk with early inoculations in order to gain early socialization of our pups. And thank goodness we did, because the damage that can be done by keeping a puppy in until fourteen weeks and more can be irreparable and affect that youngster for life. We had to take a firm line on this unpopular policy, otherwise we would never have been able to provide a sufficient number of puppies that would train on to become guide dogs. It is now over twenty years since we introduced the early inoculation policy, and thousands of puppies have been placed in homes in built-up areas across the country, with no ill effect to their health. It was a gamble, but it paid off and was undoubtedly the right thing to do.

I recently attended a Symposium with some veterinary surgeons, and they were intrigued by the inoculation procedure we had adopted over the years, and in particular with the results that we had gained with so few losses, and at the same time achieving such a high success rate of dogs with an equable temperament that were trainable and thoroughly humanised. I gave them chapter and verse, supported by statistics, and afterwards one vet said: "Well, even though you have given us all this information and all this data which can prove the value, I would personally still feel very uneasy about telling someone to take a six week old puppy on the street." I could understand the thinking and I asked her to enlarge on her fears. She said that if the puppy had got distemper or hardpad or perhaps parvovirus, the owner would come back and say that they had been advised very badly, and this worried her. There is a strong element of truth in this – but what would happen if that person returned a few months later with a puppy that had been kept in strict isolation and said: "I have got a very nervous puppy which is extremely difficult to live with," (for I know some are a nightmare to live with)? Would the vet still feel guilty that he or she had added to the owner's problems by failing to disclose that there are other vital factors to be taken into account?

It is important to bear in mind that the puppy that is allowed to go out may come into contact with disease and its immunity may be challenged. The early inoculation may give it some protection, and everything may be alright. However, you may get a sick puppy. Conversely, if you don't take the puppy out for early socialization it stands a very good chance of not reaching its full true potential. If it has not encountered other dogs, or strangers, and it has not even seen traffic, then there is a good chance that you can finish up with a dog who will be damaged temperamentally for life. I strongly feel that the owner should see both sides of the coin before they make a decision. At the end of this particular discussion it was evident the vets around the table felt this should be part of the new teaching of any young vets coming out of College.

A classic example of this lack of advice on humanisation and conditioning was evident in the case of a beautiful Golden Retriever male who turned up at dog club some years ago. It was owned by an elderly gentleman, who loved the dog dearly, but could not fully enjoy its company due to the dog's excessive nervous reactions. The dog, although happy and confident in the home and garden, was a trembling wreck if taken away from those surroundings. This reaction was the result of the owner following the vet's advice and keeping the dog securely within the home environment until vaccinations were completed. By this time the dog was nearly seventeen weeks of age, and it was already showing signs of worry if the owner attempted to take him out of the gate near to traffic, people, prams, and all the other hustle and bustle connected with an urban environment. The owner had sought advice from the vet, and was told to be patient and the dog would improve. Finally, in despair, he gave the dog sedatives prescribed by the vet, but the dog remained adamant that he would not venture out. Of course, the dog was no longer small and biddable; it had increased in size and body-weight, and the owner was forced to abandon his efforts to get it out for a walk. When the dog was twelve months old, a friend advised the owner to try a dog training club. With the help of his adult son, he managed to get their dog in the car, and together they carried it from the car to the clubhouse, and there I was presented with an 80 lbs dog and the tale of woe.

The dog sat shivering like an aspen leaf while we discussed our plan for his training and conditioning, which at this stage required a crash course that would inevitably be traumatic for him. I fitted a strong collar and lead on him, ensuring that the collar was escape-proof and double-clipped my leash. I then told the dog's handler to act as the carrot, hoping that the calls of encouragement from his owner, who was to walk a few paces ahead, would provide the incentive for the dog to follow. This worked quite well, once we got the dog moving in a quiet area, although he had learnt the art of sitting down and resisting, and was as stubborn as a donkey. By the time we hit the main road I don't know who was more shattered – me, the dog or the elderly owner – but the dog had plenty of fight left in him. As soon as the first car approached, he dived for the wall on our left, and then up and over a small privet hedge into a boarding house, leaving me spreadeagled across the hedge, gallantly holding on to the leash. All the time, the owner was calling out "good dog", which he insisted on doing, irrespective of the dog's behaviour! Finally, I retrieved the dog and got him composed, but it took very firm control to settle him down and make him overcome his innate fear of the whole world, people, and traffic. I handed him back to his owner, telling him not to let the dog dive into his garden when they got home. He should stop some way from the house and then walk the dog in the opposite direction, all the time exercising positive control, and giving lavish praise when the dog responded. When they reached the house, he should pass the gate several times before allowing the dog to enter. Then, as soon as the dog made for the front door, the owner should turn it about and take it for a further five-minute walk out of the gate and up the road, rewarding it profusely once it moved out of the gate.

This dog came to the training club for several months after that initial visit and he was a much improved dog, but he was never sound. We had to be hard on it initially to overcome its very great fear of most things; but this need never have happened, if the dog been reared well in the first place, and if the owner had received the right advice regarding the dog's need for conditioning at the critical stage, as well as its inoculation requirements.

When parvovirus arrived in the UK in the late seventies, nothing was known about the disease and its prevention, and this gave us a whole new anxiety. When it first hit the country in 1979, it was believed that if a litter was infected when it was only a few days old, the puppies would probably go down with myocarditis and they would all die. The first protective vaccine we used was one already in use for cats – the feline enteritis vaccine. We tried both 'live' and 'dead' types, and neither gave complete protection, but it was all that was available at the time, and undoubtedly saved many deaths of young pups exposed to infection.

About this time, I was on a consultative appointment, visiting a guide dog school in the USA which was experiencing 62 per cent fatality in their breeding stock as a direct result of contact with parvovirus. The school's production was severely affected for several years, forcing them to rely on gift dogs in order to supply their clients. They also had to close down their breeding unit, which was in an old farm building, as it could not easily be fumigated and cleaned. The only solution was to move to a new unit, some twenty-five miles away, which was built on more modern lines. I can only feel that we, at GDBA, were fortunate in avoiding such a distressing situation. This was largely due to the fact that we had built good isolation kennels at Tollgate, when the Breeding Centre was first established, and these proved invaluable in separating sick puppies from the rest of our stock. In Britain, a good, approved canine vaccine was imported from Australia and soon came on the market.

Fortunately, it had an immediate effect in reducing the risk of infection. Within GDBA we adopted the same policy as for distemper, with an early inoculation. The inoculation is given to six-week-old puppies and they receive another injection at twelve weeks. They then receive boosters against parvovirus at five months and one year of age.

The inoculation of breeding stock now follows a different pattern. Initially, we were told to boost brood bitches when they came in for mating and then annually. Unfortunately, we found that many bitches were producing small litters, or failing to conceive at all. Sometimes the whelps were born dead. Studs were also inoculated annually, and they sometimes seemed to have difficulty in achieving a successful mating. I felt very unhappy about the situation because the supply of puppies was affected. Eventually we changed the policy from boosting bitches when they came in to be mated to boosting them after they had finished rearing their litter. This meant the puppies in utero would not be affected by any injected vaccine, but they would acquire immunity from antibodies their dam was carrying prior to boosting.

We also stopped giving the stud dogs an annual booster against parvovirus. We now take blood samples from every male, and these are sent to Glasgow Veterinary College for assessment. We then give booster injections to the studs with a low immunity to parvovirus. Although we keep at least fifty stud dogs, only two or three need boosting regularly. Their low level of immunity, which showed up in these blood samples, is curious, as these individuals mixed with other dogs in the kennel complex and therefore must have been regularly challenged with the virus which came on the premises. The selective approach to boosting studs worked, because conception rates improved, as did the studs' ability to achieve and complete a mating.

At the worst stage of the parvovirus epidemic we lost only six older puppies at about six months of age. We also lost one full litter of seven, which was infected in the nest or at birth after a Caesarian section on the bitch; four of the puppies succumbed in the first week of life, while the remainder developed myocarditis and had to be put to sleep at about five months of age. Three stud dogs became infertile, and at the height of the crisis 32 per cent of matings failed, compared with 19 per cent previously. After the introduction of new inoculation procedures for broods and studs, fertility failure rates were brought down to 15 per cent, which is more acceptable. During and after the parvovirus phase, we had 200 brood bitches and conducted about 300 matings per year (each bitch being mated twice over 48 hours). In homes as far apart as Exeter, London, the Midlands, the North East and the North West of England, and Scotland, we had a total of 750 puppies on the puppy walking scheme. Kennel cough has been about for a long time, but we were not too worried about the occasional dog that went down with it; the harsh, dry cough was very persistent and irritating, and it might last a few or more weeks. Then suddenly, the cough infection pattern altered. Entire kennel blocks of dogs would go down with it, and instead of it being found only in boarding and training kennels, it began to affect dogs which had been to shows and sometimes pets which had been exercised in parks or on commons used by other dogs. In 1978 the cough was so bad in the Leamington Training Centre that a whole class of blind students had to be deferred for over a month until the epidemic died down and training could be resumed. Protection against this sort of disaster was clearly desirable, but we were offered little hope by the main manufacturers of dog vaccines in the UK. We heard that there was a vaccine under development, but all we could do was wait. Summer after summer, we expended all our energy in trying to keep the cough out of kennels, isolating and treating any dog that was heard to cough. At last Mycofarm launched the Intrac 1 kennel cough vaccine, which was a completely new method of protection. They had taken a living virulent strain of the Bordetalla bronchia-septica bacteria and prepared it as a vaccine to be given as drops up the dog's nose. The vaccine worked by stimulating local immunity in the nose and throat, and was supposed to stop infection reaching the trachea and lungs, where it was difficult to cure. Their other vaccine, Intrac 2, was also administered as nose drops, and this gave protection against para-influenza as well as Bordetella in the first vaccine.

When we introduced the vaccine, we understood that it did not stop all coughs. However, treatment was easy and quick, and trials in other kennels showed that unvaccinated dogs with the cough took an average of twelve days to cure, compared with only six days for a vaccinated dog. Kennel cough vaccine has become more popular, as a way of protecting dogs, over the last few years, and most boarding kennels request that dogs must have received the vaccine before accepting them. We were rather careful about using kennel cough vaccine at the Breeding Centre, because we wanted to reassure ourselves there would be no side-effects. In fact, some of the Training Centres pioneered it before it came to us. This turned out to be a wise precaution, for later one of the two vaccines was withdrawn. I believe this was because of side-effects, although our Training Centres had not experienced any problems. The general opinion from the Training Centres was that perhaps it had a value, and this was when the two-component vaccine was available; one was against para-influenza and the other against Bordetella bronchi-septica. The difficulty we encountered at the Breeding Centre, when we started using it, was that there appeared to be some variation in the disease from one year to the next, and this appeared to affect the protection gained from using the vaccines. When one of the two varieties of the vaccine was eventually withdrawn, we were left with Interac on the market, which gives protection only against Bordetella bronchia-septica. Consequentally, the first step when encountering a cough in a kennel environment is to discover which form of the virus or bacteria it is. The other problem for the puppy unit was that it was better to administer the vaccine to the puppy two to five weeks before it came into kennels. However, this was an almost impossible task, with puppies often coming into kennels at short notice. We attempted to establish a policy, but to add to our problems, the shelf-life of the product was only about six months, and many of the vets in the areas where we have puppies, had to order special supplies of it. They therefore needed early notification of our requirements, which were not always predictable.

1986 was the first full year we used cough vaccine, and in fact, it was in the middle of that year that we had the highest number of coughing dogs on the premises! We had twenty-seven coughing puppies in our isolation block, and they were there for a very long time, as they took a long time to recover. The pet owner can keep a dog in total isolation, but in our situation, it seemed that by keeping the affected puppies in a group in the isolation block, with other pups joining them, we were constantly refuelling the fire, and the problem kept going round and round as dogs became reinfected. I could only presume that the dogs were being affected by a virulent new virus, possibly para-influenza strains, or we were not inoculating all puppies early enough, prior to kenneling. Fortunately, the cough does not result in serious longterm damage. We have never actually lost a puppy through kennel cough, but it is a nuisance. I am very loath to send puppies home coughing, because they may infect other dogs in their home area, as the germs are spread on water droplets coughed into the atmosphere.

The administration of vaccine is normally only given by a qualified vet, when a vaccination certificate is issued. A very limited number of nominated guide dog staff are now permitted to give kennel cough boosters to the dogs owned by GDBA, while they are on the puppy-walking scheme in order to vaccinate puppies well in advance of them entering kennels. In the past it was hoped that a wider range of staff could give any inoculations in the kennels, but now the Medicines Act, has prevented this, tighteneing up these procedures tremendously. The law states that you can treat your own dog, providing it is not proved to be cruel to do so. The special arrangement for GDBA staff to give booster inoculations is certainly a help, but I feel there is still a need for a vaccine to protect against para-influenza and any other similar viruses, and I was sorry that Interac II was withdrawn from sale and not replaced.

The normal route for giving most vaccine injections is subcutaneous, which means it goes under the skin. Nowadays, it is administered from a sterile and disposable plastic syringe, though I can recall vets coming round with a little tin box containing a metal syringe. All you could do was hope it had been sterilised after being used on the last animal. I used to wonder where they managed to boil the water, then I realised that unlike today's vets who drive around in BMWs and Range Rovers, most veterinarians had old bangers which gave them a convenient reservoir of boiling-hot water!

I had a reputation among my staff for claiming that dogs do not experience pain when they are injected. However, I was caught out a number of years ago when I was at the Leamington Training Centre. A guide dog owner was in the dispensary, and I was due to inoculate a whole litter of puppies which had just arrived on the premises. The guide dog owner was a bit squeamish and wondered if she should leave, but I merrily assured her that there was no need, for puppies normally accept the inoculation without any adverse response at all. Needless to say, these were famous last words! There were ten puppies and every one of them protested loudly. This was most unusual, and in fact these particular puppies were of relatively high body and mental sensitivity and grew up to be well on the edge of the tolerances required. They were extremely sensitive animals with acute mental response.

GDBA INOCULATION POLICY

0-6 weeks	Natural immunity from mother	In nest with dam
6-7 weeks	Distemper, hardpad, leptospirosis, hepatitis & parvovirus. Placed in home with puppy walker	
12 weeks	Distemper, hardpad, leptospirosis, hepatitis & parvovirus. With puppy walker.	
14 weeks	Leptospirosis booster. With puppy walker	
20 weeks	Parvovirus booster. With puppy walker.	
10-14 months	Full booster given *(Kennel cough vaccine given 5 weeks prior to entering kennels)	
(exception pregnant broods)	To a training centre or breeding centre.	
Every 12 months	Full booster	Qualified guide dog

After a litter   Full booster   Brood bitches

Every 12 months   Distemper, hardpad, leptospirosis
                         & hepatitis. parvovirus as indicated by titre counts.   Stud
                         dogs

Chapter Eleven

QUESTIONS AND ANSWERS ON TRAINING

When a litter is born at our Breeding Centre we start a health record card for each puppy, and check their progress regularly. Kennel staff handle and talk to the pups daily, and eventually wean, feed, groom, play with, and discipline over-vigorous pups. Staff encourage their charges to respond to the voice and they gain a thorough knowledge of the character of each pup. This information is invaluable in selecting the best homes for them.

At six to seven weeks old the puppies leave either the brood bitch owner's home, or our whelping kennels at Tollgate House, to go out on the puppy-walking scheme, where they will be walked, under supervision, by their adopted parents, the puppy walkers, until they are about twelve months old. Some come in a little earlier, at ten months, but breeds like the German Shepherd, which mature much slower, are left until they are fourteen months old. During the puppy-walking period, the males are castrated, usually between seven to twelve months, according to sexual drive. The bitches are invariably spayed after their second season, during their time at the Training Centres, which is on average at about sixteen months of age. Potential breeding stock will already have been identified while at walk, and at the end of puppy walking these will be directed to the breeding unit; others with good potential as guide dogs are distributed to the various Training Centres, where for some forty-plus weeks they will be trained. At about two years old they "pass out" as guide dogs.

Detailed reports on each puppy at walk are essential in order to keep track-records of the individual studs and broods. Monthly reports are written by the supervisors on the spot, and there is a feedback from each centre on the attitude and progress of all puppies in training. We never expect all puppies initially placed on the puppy-walking scheme to make it as guide dogs, and on average 78 per cent will finish the training successfully or join the breeding stock. The unsuccessful dogs usually go to selected homes as pets, and we have a waiting list of people hoping to have our rejects. Others may go to other working-dog organisations such as the Royal Air Force, Police, Customs, and Prison Service. Some are donated to hospitals and hospices up and down the country, and to Hearing Dogs and Dogs for the Disabled.

During puppy walking there are a number of training and behavioural problems that may be encountered, and over the years we have developed methods of dealing with a number of these. This knowledge has proved invaluable, as once a problem has been spotted in a dog, the puppy walker can be advised on the the correct approach.

QUESTION: How do you correct puppies with a left tendency?

ANSWER: In an ideal situation, a guide dog puppy should walk in the centre of the pavement with the handler slightly behind, termed right of centre. In some situations, where the main road is on the right and there is very heavy traffic, it is permissible, in order to keep a dog reassured, for it to move slightly over to the left. However, we do not want a pup which scrapes against a wall on the left when the road is on its right or, conversely, hogs the kerb edge. I see many dog owners with pets who have developed this problem. Left tendency is often seen in the early stages of puppy walking, particularly in puppies of a sensitive nature who are walked in heavy traffic areas. The reaction may be caused by the proximity of traffic, or the noise of traffic. However, it can also be a reaction of the animal to its handler. The handler may be keeping the puppy on a tight leash and not allowing it flight distance in order to feel secure, and not giving it confidence by vocal encouragement at the correct time. In other words, the problems may be due to mishandling the puppy. A puppy may want to walk along the building-line and at a distance from the handler for several reasons: fear of the handler, both physical and vocal, or because of the attractive smells which can be found, such as urine from other dogs and the smell of food from shops. If the puppy is purely attracted by smells, the handler, when the problem arises, should turn around and encourage the puppy to walk in the opposite direction, with the buildings on the other side of the pup. It should be encouraged to walk ahead, leaving the attractive scents at some distance. Praise should be given effusively once the desired response has been obtained. If the puppy tries to cross in front of the handler to get to the building-line, the leash should be taken away from it slightly, jerking the pup to the left and back in a straight line. This action should be done simultaneously with the command "no".

Many puppies show signs of flight tendencies if they are faced with traffic that is fast-moving in very close proximity. Therefore it is advisable, initially, to avoid traffic on fast main roads and, indeed, down village streets if traffic moves quickly and pavements are narrow or non-existent. Go into town where traffic is slower and denser, so that the puppy can get used to it. This gives it time to listen to the encouraging voice of its handler, without being afraid of sudden rushes of noise and turbulence caused by speeding vehicles. We have found over the years that many potentially traffic-shy puppies improve in these circumstances. Never force a sensitive pup to sit at a kerb and endure traffic that is a worry to it.

A number of years ago Lt. Col. E. W. B. Harte, who was a member of our Council and a voluntary supervisor of puppies in the Hampshire area, discovered a little gold-mine of a village in Hampshire where there were a number of people willing to walk puppies. However, it was noticed after a while that a lot of the puppies placed in that village were becoming traffic-shy by the time they were about five months of age. The reason was that the village had a fast main road through it and very narrow pavements, and the puppies were reacting to the many cars that whizzed past. To overcome the problem, we asked a number of the walkers to stop taking the pups regularly into the village and to get them into the large town of Basingstoke, where traffic was heavy and dense, but moved slowly. All those puppies made remarkable progress and eventually they could cope with the fast-moving traffic in the village and elsewhere.

QUESTION: Can body-conditioning help a dog overcome the problem of a dog walking left of the handler?

ANSWER: Yes, if done humanely through the leash and voice, and not by inducing

Training starts a soon as a puppy is placed with a puppy walker.   *G. Purser.*

fear of the handler through over-correcting with the leash. A trainer from an overseas school told me that they tackle the problem by selecting a certain training area in the town where there are cast-iron fire hydrants and traffic signposts on the pavement. The dog would be walked quickly down the pavement, and if it was reluctant to come in close, it would be smartly pushed into one or two of the obstacles with the handler's knee – thus conveying the message that it was far less painful to walk close than to have a tussle with a cast-iron post. This method may or may not get the desired result with a tough dog, but it would certainly over-stress most of our present-day stock and, quite rightly, it would not be tolerated in the United Kingdom by GDBA or the general public. We prefer to advocate stroking and regular patting of the dog to encourage it to come in close.

QUESTION: A potential guide dog should put a certain amount of tension on the leash, but how do you correct a pulling dog?

ANSWER: Many puppies are inclined to do this when they are first put on a collar and leash. The puppy needs to learn that the leash and collar are not a means of punishment, but a pleasant way of walking which, when it is in the right position with the right tension, will produce encouragement and praise from the handler. Puppies are pretty astute in learning this, providing care is taken. Continual jagging with a chain check-collar is not the correct way. A check-collar can be used, but a leather slip collar is much better. Then, as soon as the puppy starts pulling too much, the leash should be flicked back – a knack that is soon acquired. At the same time the handler should give the command "steady". It is important to praise the puppy when it is in the correct position and doing the right thing.

When a puppy is going for a walk, a routine of discipline or door-drill sets up the right working atmosphere of control and praise. The pup should learn to halt and sit at each door, as you leave the house ready for the walk. If you establish control at the start of each walk, this will help to prevent the puppy from pulling. It is wrong to reward your pup with a free run when he has pulled you all the way to the park. Voice intonation and timing are all-important to encourage the puppy to listen. As soon as it starts moving out on to the end of the leash to start pulling, it should hear, in a reprimanding tone, the word "steady" and understand that it will be followed by a slightly unpleasant correction from the leash through the collar. If this is done consistently and it is correctly timed, a puppy will soon learn to come back into position. There are other ways to control pulling, and a device known as a "haltie" can help. However, it can have an off-putting effect because it resembles a muzzle.

One or two cases of pulling dogs have been brought to me for training, not from our puppy-walking scheme, but from dog clubs, where the animals had been continually, but ineffectively, jagged with chain collars and resistance had developed through the dog developing low body sensitivity. The neck of one dog was completely bare, and correction through the leash and collar only made it over-anxious and more inclined to pull in order to get away from the handler. A different approach was needed, so I took the dog out for a long walk and give it the full length of the leash. I allowed it to pull, and it would have carried on pulling indefinitely. During the walk I selected from the hedgerow a small, thin, willow twig with two leaves on the end, to act as an extension on my arm, and when the dog was pulling I gently tapped him on the nose, giving the word of command "steady", thus directing him back alongside me. After doing this several times the dog quickly responded, and as soon as the twig came in front of him he would move back alongside me, at the same time responding to my vocal request "steady" and the reward "good boy" when he achieved the correct tension. He quickly learned that the most comfortable walking position was alongside my leg, and we did a six mile walk on that first day, with no pulling. I used the twig on three occasions, in order to tap him back. On other occasions I used it to stroke and caress him. From then on, I took him out daily round the six mile circuit, and on the fourth day I threw the twig away. The dog had learned to walk sensibly ahead, with slight tension, and to respond to voice. It knew exactly what "steady" meant, and that "good boy, up, up" was meant to encourage him out in front to get slight tension. Each and every day he was happy to come out walking with me, and he had no desire to pull incessantly, as he had no fear of leash, collar or handler.

QUESTION: If a dog pulls, is it is either trying to get to, or get away from, somebody or something?

Answer: It is true that most pulling dogs can be placed in these two categories. Either they are over-enthusiastic in their desire to achieve their chosen object – a walk in the park, another dog or the smell of food; or they are pulling to get away from their handler, usually prompted by fear. If you can diagnose why a dog is pulling, you have already done a lot towards overcoming the problem.

QUESTION: What is crab-walk, and what can be done about it?

ANSWER: This is when the dog is constantly looking up at its handler and moves in a sideways, crab-like fashion. It is usually caused through over-handling, and it is difficult to overcome. Invariably puppies or adults of a sensitive nature develop it through being over-corrected, either physically or verbally. I have seen it in a large number of obedience dogs that have, in my estimation, been trained to be over-attentive and need to concentrate on the expression and body language of their handler. The way to overcome the problem is to encourage the puppy or dog to walk out ahead on a leash so that it can't possibly react to expressions or body movements of the handler. Gradually, after a period of walking with the dog at the end of a long leash, encourage it back by reclaiming the leash until it is walking in the correct position, just slightly ahead of the handler.

In obedience, one of the best ways of overcoming crab-walking is to repeatedly do left turns into the dog, because then the dog has to move away from you to make distance. It must be done carefully, of course, because if the dog gets trampled on, it could aggravate the problem rather than ease it. I recommend prolonged walking-out on a long leash as the best method known to me of overcoming any crabbing tendency.

QUESTION: How do you deal with positive dog distraction – the dog that lunges forward and takes a marked and sometimes aggressive interest in other dogs or cats?

ANSWER: Most puppies, if they have been conditioned properly to meet other dogs, cats, animals and birds, will show no sign of hostility towards them; as they are confident about meeting or passing them. During the time a puppy is out at walk, it should be allowed to meet other dogs and make their acquaintance. It is important that no set pattern is established: on some occasions, the puppy should be encouraged to walk past and ignore a dog, and on other occasions it should be allowed stop and talk to a dog, and then walk past the next four or five dogs, so that the puppy is continually reacting and responding to the voice or command of the handler. If the puppy starts showing hostility towards other dogs it should be immediately corrected by simultaneous signal and command, both vocal and physical, and told to move ahead.

I believe that, depending on the sensitivity and size of the puppy, it should be corrected quite firmly, for I do not believe that half-measures have much value but only worry and confuse. Puppies should, as soon as possible, be given the opportunity of meeting other animals while they are under full control, and be told to enquire, then move away. The handler should make every effort to ensure that the response from the puppy is immediate, without the puppy becoming anxious or hostile. A good spontaneous reaction should be rewarded immediately by vocal and physical praise.

QUESTION: How do you correct negative dog distraction – when the dog shies away from another dog or cat through fear, but would give chase if the opponent took flight?

ANSWER: The puppy should be given the opportunity to meet and play with other animals that are extremely confident with young puppies. I believe there is a value in taking young puppies to dog clubs, providing the dogs they meet at the clubs are of an ideal temperament. Be careful, however, that your pup does not meet the dog that always seems to be under the chair at the entrance to almost every club. This is the dog that is prepared to take on all-comers and has an idiot for an owner, who selects the one spot it should not occupy. The puppy that shows signs of negative dog distraction ought to be given plenty of opportunity to meet friendly, out-going dogs, to free-run and play with them, and never to feel challenged.

The same would apply with cats. Any puppy showing signs of worry or concern about cats should be brought into close contact with a friendly cat. Great strides can be made by doing this regularly while the puppy is very young. It is obviously better still if you have a cat at home. They are a lot easier to house-train than dogs, and they don't require walking in the rain!

QUESTION: What do you do about a dog that walks behind its handler?

ANSWER: Lagging puppies are very difficult to deal with. It does not necessarily mean that the puppy is tired or reluctant to leave the home, although these are valid reasons. Try to establish why the puppy is not happy about walking out ahead or going for a pleasant walk. I have known numerous puppies that wanted to go for a walk as soon as the collar and lead had been put on, yet when they got out on the pavement they immediately dropped behind. In several cases we noticed that these puppies showed signs of limping, a problem which I deal with in a later chapter.

If the puppy is just being a 'mummy's darling' and is reluctant to leave home, the best thing to do is to take it a little distance from home in a vehicle, and then walk it back to the house. Invariably, the puppy will then walk ahead immediately, and as soon as it does it should be given the correct words of "up, up, good dog", when it is in the right position. Some puppies put the brakes on when a leash and collar are first introduced. In order to overcome this, leave the leash attached to the collar then, go to the kitchen, make up the puppy's meal and rattle the dishes, and this will encourage the puppy to walk with both leash and collar attached. You can extend the distance the puppy walks by moving the food bowl about the house.

Some years ago, at the request of an experienced walker, I went down to Surrey to see a German Shepherd puppy. His name was Vallis, and he eventually became a very good guide dog and worked with one of our regional organisers for many years. I heard that the puppy, who was very large and eight or nine months of age, was reluctant to go out for a walk when the puppy walker got the leash down to exercise him. Vallis would wag his tail when the puppy walker went to the leash, but once the leash was in the puppy walker's hand and the collar was ready to put on, he would retreat under the dining-room table with his ears back.

While I was having a cup of tea with the puppy walker, Vallis sat attentively watching us both, knowing full well that normally when I visited the house we went for a walk, and he looked eager and excited, just like any other puppy. The walker said: "Watch his reaction now," and he got up and went into the kitchen. Vallis went with him, wagging his tail, but when the puppy walker lifted the collar down from the hook, he dived straight under the table in the living room, showing all signs of anxiety and worry. The puppy walker assured me that he had not beaten the dog, because that was the impression it gave. I believed him, because I had known him and his dogs for many years. However, this dog was certainly concerned about what was going on. Fortunately I had a leather slip collar in the car, and I asked him to replace the chain collar on the hook with the leather slip and give me the chain collar, which I placed in my pocket. We sat talking for a further five minutes while we drank another cup of tea, then I asked him to go through the procedure again. Vallis reacted in the same manner, looking eager to go out for a walk and wagging his tail when the leash was taken down. When the walker picked up the collar the dog's ears started to go down, but there was no determined rush to get under the table. He stood and looked perplexed. When the leather slip was put on and the leash clipped to it, the dog was all keyed up to go out.

"That is what he used to be like," said the walker. "Why should he react in an adverse manner to the other collar?" The answer was that the chain collar was the wrong type of collar for such a sensitive pup. It was a big, heavy-duty chain collar, far too cumbersome and far too harsh for the dog in question, although his size and colour made him appear like a more tough and rugged dog.

QUESTION: What should be done about the stubborn dog, which may have shown protective aggression as a youngster?

ANSWER: Stubborn dogs do not normally finish up as guide dogs. If the puppy is over-dominant, under-sensitive, and hostile as well, it is obviously the wrong type for us. However, in the early days of my career we did train a number of such dogs, and I regret to say that the only method of getting through to dogs of this nature is by harsh physical handling. The make-up of a dog like this is more suited to attack work or something similar, where low body sensitivity can be used to the full.

QUESTION: What can be done about a destructive puppy?

ANSWER: All puppies need to be occupied, particularly when they are beginning to lose their first teeth and get their second dentition. Normally their main occupation at that time is chewing, both to give vent to their feelings and also to assist in cutting their second teeth. If the puppy at this time is deprived of its own toys, it will find substitutes in the form of household equipment, furnishings and fittings. It is therefore important to give the puppy numerous toys – a puppy gets bored with the same toy all the time – but be careful to select playthings that cannot be swallowed.

If you have to leave a puppy for any length of time, make sure it has a chance to relieve itself, and is put in an area or room where it can do the least damage. Make sure that the puppy has plenty of toys, even an empty cardboard box, for it is better that the puppy vents its feelings on the box, rather than on your new three-piece suite. All puppies need educating about being left on their own in the early stages. It is unfair to indulge your puppy for weeks on end with your constant company, and then suddenly to leave it. This causes separation anxiety, and can be avoided by conditioning your puppy to spending a small time on his own initially, and lengthening the time as your puppy gets older.

While the puppy is being reared it must not be allowed to pick up articles other than its own toys. Even last week's newspaper must be given up and replaced with a toy. Time should be spent with the puppy encouraging it to play with toys, because to laugh at a puppy that is destroying last week's newspaper or chewing an old slipper is tantamount to encouraging it, next week, to chew the *Encyclopaedia Britannica* or your best pair of shoes. Therefore, consistency at all times is important, to ensure the puppy knows what it is allowed to play with.

QUESTION: Are some breeds more prone to destructive behaviour than others?

ANSWER: Some breeds are certainly more destructive than others, with the Labrador at the top of the list for destructiveness during the early stages of development. They are an enquiring breed and they like carrying objects in their mouths, as do Golden Retrievers, but Labradors are possibly a little more robust. Every puppy can be taught good behaviour, providing you are available and willing to educate it. A number of years ago I saw two surveys carried out by guide dog schools in America. They found that German Shepherds were the least destructive through the rearing period, Golden Retrievers were more destructive, and Labradors were the worst.

American schools and dog trainers advocate the use of an indoor wire kennel to accommodate the puppy in your absence, but we have not used them extensively. The idea is to allow the puppy free access in and out of the kennel during the time you are at home, so that initially it looks upon the kennel, or cage, as its sanctuary or bed. Toys and other delicacies to chew can be put in there, so the puppy feels relaxed and happy in the environment. At first, the kennel door should only be closed for short periods of time, clipping the latch on the door to lock the puppy securely in the cage, where it can do no mischief. The puppy should never think of the cage as a place of punishment by being sent to it when it has transgressed. It should be allowed free range of the home when you are in, and it should not be locked in the cage for long periods. The puppy should never be let out when it is protesting, for this would be equivalent to rewarding it for bad behaviour. The puppy should only be allowed out when it has quietened down, and it should then be rewarded.

QUESTION: What can you do about a puppy that forms an especially deep attachment to its walker?

ANSWER: This is the type of puppy which often lags when it goes out, because it is reluctant to walk away from the home to which it is attached. The ideal treatment, once the problem has been identified, is to encourage the walker to allow the puppy to be taken out and walked by other members of the household, or by a responsible friend or relative. If the puppy can be accommodated for a couple of days by different people, it can help the puppy to break the attachment. If none of this is possible, or is not available often enough to be able to make a mark on the puppy, then invariably we advocate that the puppy comes into kennels for what we call a kennel break. The length of the break will depend on the severity of the individual's problem. This kennel break is invaluable to some pups: it teaches them to be confident and not over-dependent.

   A puppy that is coming into kennels for this reason must be housed with dogs of its own size and sensitivity, so that it is not bullied. Ideally, we accommodate it with other puppies that are friendly, and we ensure that it is regularly walked out on a leash in pleasant surroundings. It does not have to be town surroundings, so long as it gains confidence and becomes relaxed about being walked by different handlers.

QUESTION: What can be done about a puppy that is worried by noise and bustle in places such as railway or bus stations?

ANSWER: Take the puppy on a regular daily visit to the bus or railway station. Do not enter into the very thick of activity at first, but stay on the edge so that the puppy can become accustomed to the environment. Let it hear trains in the distance, and reward it with voice and titbits for improved behaviour. After several visits, when the puppy is becoming relaxed, take it a little further into busier surroundings, always reassuring it with confident handling and firm direction.

QUESTION: How do you cope with a puppy that is a poor traveller?

ANSWER: Many puppies have adverse reactions to car and bus travel, and usually it is the more sensitive puppies that react the worst. A great deal can be done to overcome this problem by increasing the puppy's confidence. Start by feeding the puppy in the well of a car without the engine running, and then progress to feeding it with the engine running. Make frequent car journeys to nearby free-running areas, with the puppy in the passenger-well, being controlled, not consoled, by a passenger. Try to meet friends with canine companions at the free-running area – the puppy will soon realise the pleasure that follows a journey. Do not give the puppy food or water before journeys. Eventually, go on several long journeys with someone the puppy is confident with, and have the puppy in direct physical contact, not trapped in the rear of vehicle in isolation. When you are travelling by bus, condition the puppy in a similar manner, first travelling only one or two bus stops and then walking home; lengthen the journeys as the puppy's confidence grows. Avomine travel tablets can be useful, but I prefer to condition the puppy over a period of time.

It is important to bear in mind, when teaching a puppy or dog a new procedure or exercise, that most puppies and adult dogs do things willingly if they derive a pleasant sensation or benefit from the exercise. They will cease to do things willingly if they derive an unpleasant, painful or distasteful experience. However, armed with this knowledge, many novice or forceful handlers are inclined to work on the negative aspects rather than the positive inducements, and the result can be a very submissive, unwilling, and in some cases, belligerent dog. As a teacher, you have to set certain rules for yourself: mine are to be consistent and persistent, to make the exercise as simple as possible and to build steadily, always finishing training on a successful and happy note. Timing is very important in order to get the correct response. When your puppy knows you are pleased and it knows it will be rewarded, either vocally (praise), physically (patting), or occasionally with a titbit, it will want to do things for you, for it is also gaining pleasure.

Intonation of voice is all-important to stimulate a puppy into the correct act or posture, or alternatively, to dissuade him from doing the wrong thing. The voice used in this way should be like a water tap, easy to turn on or off; and timing in relation to response is all-important. A firm tone should be used for an exercise such as 'drop' or 'down', and care should be taken not to excite the puppy when you are asking it to stand or stay. When you are training your puppy the environment is most important: initially there should be minimum distractions. Distractions may be added once a puppy or dog fully understands what is expected.

In my experience, I have seen very few mentally defective dogs, but I have seen very many confused dogs, and they usually live with inconsistent, over-tolerant owners, who love their dog to excess. These owners are unable to understand why, when the puppy matures, he is over-demanding, disobedient and even aggressive. Dogs are pack animals and look upon the family they live with as being their pack, and as they mature and become established, they strive to improve their status, which with a well-schooled dog is lower than the human. If your dog is one who has taken over the bed or the settee, and fights you to be first at the door when visitors arrive or when it is to be taken for a walk, it is taking over your role as head of the pack.

With proper socialization and education, your puppy should respect you and expect affection from you as pack leader. Both respect and affection are equally important, and they should be balanced. Affection given for no good reason is valueless, and it reduces the impact when it is given for the right reason. The same is equally true of correction. You should aim at having a dog who listens and responds to your voice and body movements, one that is a joy to own and live with, and that tells you so – and everyone else – by its happy and uncomplicated disposition.

Part III

Health Care

Chapter Twelve

THE CASE FOR NEUTERING

When I first came to GDBA, I had very strong feelings about the spaying of bitches and at the end of the fifties the operation was seldom performed on guide dogs. Occasionally, a bitch would be spayed if there was a strong request from the guide dog owner. Few males were being used at that time, and they were usually not castrated. At the time, I felt that neutering was a little barbaric and probably unkind to the dogs. As I had joined the Association very much with the interests of dogs in mind, I felt that to subject them to this operation once they were trained was possibly a little unjust.

In the early sixties an incident occurred that made me think differently. I was out supervising and canvassing for puppy walkers in the Birmingham area with a puppy-walking supervisor, when we saw a guide dog owner whose bitch was being harassed by a male Collie. The dog was trying to mount the working guide dog bitch, and the guide dog owner was doing his best to drive the animal off by threatening it with his white stick, at the same time encouraging his guide dog to lead him to the shops. We pulled up, and I jumped out of the car. I knew the guide dog owner because he had recently trained with his new dog at the Leamington Training Centre, and while I was speaking to him the Collie was still doing its utmost to mount the bitch, who was obviously in full season. The bitch was under great stress, trying to protect herself, and I recall saying to the guide dog owner, "Could you not have left your dog at home and gone to the shops with the white stick?" He replied that three times that morning he had attempted to get to the shops without his dog, but he had become upset and frustrated and had to return home. At one time he could get about with a stick, but since having a guide dog he found the stick exceedingly stressful. "I realise it is not ideal for the bitch, but what am I to do?" he asked. I suggested he should ask the Association to have the bitch spayed, particularly as he had to work in areas where there were numerous stray dogs.

The incident with the Collie ended after I noticed that it did not like loud noises. I asked the guide dog owner if his dog was alright with loud bangs, and after being assured that she was "bomb proof", I took a starting pistol from the car, checked to ensure there were no other people to startle and that no cars were approaching, and then emptied the magazine behind the Collie. It immediately decided that discretion was the better part of valour, and beat a hasty retreat down the road. After that I realised that although I held very strong views about spaying, there were occasions that totally justified it. Some months later I noticed that the guide dog bitch was in our hospital block awaiting the operation. I spoke to the dog's owner later still, after the bitch had been working for a number of years, and by which time it had become policy for all guide dogs to be neutered. He told me what a difference the spaying had made. They were now able to move around freely without fear of the sort of incident I had witnessed.

This explains why we neuter our bitches – but why castrate the males? They do not come into season and consequently do not present such a problem. This is true to a certain extent, but it could be argued that a vigorous entire male is always in season and is stimulated by the smell of bitches in season. Another important factor is that males working as guide dogs are likely to be challenged in built-up areas where other male dogs roam. The problem disappears if the guide dog is neutered because he then presents no threat to other dogs and, of course, is less interested in the opposite sex or in the scent they exude in the height of the season.

GDBA now neuters all working guide dogs, male and female. The male is normally castrated as he is becoming mature. The exact timing will depend on his sex drive and sensitivity, but the operation is usually carried out when the dog is between seven and ten months or age. Bitches are usually spayed when they are in training, at approximately twelve to eighteen months of age, after they have had their first season. One big advantage of having a bitch spayed, apart from the risk of having puppies, is that the risk of a mammary tumour is reduced to almost nil. Bitches that have seasons twice a year can get mammary cancers in middle or old age, but when they are spayed these seldom arise. Spaying also eliminates false pregnancy problems.

There are reasons other than the obvious one for castrating dogs. It helps to prevent disease and excessive male behaviour. Fighting isn't a great problem with potential guide dogs, but some subtle inter-male dominance can be discouraged, if not stopped entirely, by castration. Dogs have memories and they learn male behaviour which persists even after the testicles have been removed. This is why we try to get our dogs castrated as early as possible. Castrated dogs can mate with a bitch on heat but, of course, with castration, the dog is infertile. Dogs can still show signs of wanting to fight, but usually the intensity of the attack is reduced and may be no more than the ritual display of baring teeth and growling. It is not unknown for the uncastrated older dog to develop painful prostate gland enlargement – a problem which rarely affects a castrated dog.

Chapter Thirteen

HEALTH AND NUTRITION

There are a great many differences of opinion and practice on the subject of feeding dogs. I can only speak from my own experience of being responsible for the rearing of many thousands of puppies, over the years. There are always well over eight hundred GDBA puppies being raised in the homes of our puppy walkers, at any one time. The majority will eventually emerge as mature, trainable animals, and some 75 per cent will eventually become guide dogs.

It is most important that the right type of nourishment is given to the puppy at all stages of its development – indeed, throughout its life. Our approach to feeding has varied over the many years that we have been breeding and rearing animals. The dog, I firmly believe, is a carnivorous animal. Some people say it is not purely carnivorous because, given the opportunity, it will eat the entrails of herbaceously-fed animals, grass or vegetation. That may be true, but if a dog eats any of this food in any quantity, it will act as a medicine or emetic for the dog. I still firmly believe that the dog is a carnivore, and that proof can be found in its teeth. The early teeth are, of course, milk teeth which deal with the softer type of food. The food that the puppy would be dealing with in the wild would be the milk from its mother and then regurgitated food that she would be bring back to the litter – all of which is soft feeding. Once puppy teeth have gone, at five to six months of age, they are replaced by a full set of adult teeth, usually forty-two in number. Four of these are canines that assist in hunting, catching, holding and killing prey. At the front of the mouth there are twelve incisors (six each at the top and bottom), and in the wild these would be used for stripping the carcass. Behind the incisors there are twenty-six pre-molars and molars, which are used for grinding and cutting.

In my experience, a dog thrives best when it is given foodstuffs that enable it to use its teeth, according to their proper function, on a regular basis, thus keeping them clean at the same time. In a domesticated dog the canines are of little use because we provide for the dog, rather than allowing it to catch and kill. However, if you feed carcasses, sheep's heads or breasts of mutton, the dog will use canines to catch, the incisors to strip and the pre-molars and molars for cutting and grinding. In the process, the dog's mouth is kept clean and his breath sweet. I feel very strongly that this is the type of food best suited to all medium to large-size adult dogs, and this is the basis of the system of feeding that we have evolved over the years.

At six weeks old a puppy goes on to the puppy-walking scheme, and it is initially fed puppy biscuit of a good quality – normally wheatmeal biscuits. There are some puppies and adults that cannot deal with the wheat in this type of biscuit, and in those cases we would change to one which was not made of wheatmeal. At first, the six to ten-week-old puppies are fed the biscuit with minced meat, and they gradually progress to chunks of meat. If we cannot get that type of food, a good quality brand of tinned food is used which contains more roughage than many of the high protein brands. It is also cheaper. At this stage, our puppies are on four feeds a day, meat and biscuit alternating with a cereal feed such as Weetabix, dry rusks or wholemeal bread. By six to seven months, they are down to two meals a day, but this very much depends upon the individual. At this age the second teeth will have arrived, and the puppy should be receiving a diet that will help him to keep his teeth clean, his breath sweet, and his digestive tract active. I recommend raw bones as part of the diet, but definitely not cooked bones Good quality raw bones have been found to be good for young puppies and adult stock, but they should not be counted as an extra meal; they should be given in addition to other food. Feeding remains unchanged until the puppy is approaching maturity, usually at ten to eighteen months, depending upon the breed. Gradually, the number of feeds can be reduced, and the volume of each meal can be increased according to the individual's needs until it is down to one or two feeds at around eighteen months of age. Most guide dogs in training require two meals a day of meat and biscuits.

By the time they have reached maturity, most dogs should be on one feed a day of meat and biscuit. Raw meat should be offered in large chunks, a minimum of 1lb to 2lb given with biscuit. The proportion should vary according to the dog. For example, Labradors, are able to convert food well, so they normally need a smaller proportion of biscuit than most guide dogs of comparable age and weight. Knacker meat can be used but, by law, it must be lightly cooked. We have fed this successfully over many years, but we are very selective in what we purchase, avoiding carcasses from animals that have been very diseased. Almost all our knacker meat is casualty meat. A suitable substitute is breast of mutton, which should be fed raw and on the bone. Some puppies find difficulty in dealing with the fat content if it is too fatty, but the majority are able to cope with it. Breast of mutton is very cheap and usually available, particularly in summer months. Another economical food is sheep's heads, although nowadays these are very difficult to get hold of. We feed them raw, although I should emphasise that we scoop the brains out before giving them to the dog, because of the risk of tapeworm infection. They are ideal for making stock for feeding litters and their nursing dams. Care should be taken not to feed with too much skin on, in case the animal has recently been dipped. Any regurgitated grass should be cleaned out from the nose and throat, otherwise your dog will be sick. Before they start their training all our dogs will have been given this type of diet. Typically, they will have maintained good body weight, good condition, and will not have needed to have their teeth scaled.

When I first joined the Association it was a ritual that every young adult had to have its teeth scaled before going into training. They were barely fourteen months of age. Feeding at that time was wheat biscuit soaked in water, made into almost a pulp, which was the manufacturer's recommendation. I would describe it as sludge. Minced meat was fed raw, and was again a sloppy pulp. Needless to say, the vast majority of dogs that we had at the time had foul breath and dirty (or, more exactly, filthy) teeth, which needed cleaning at this early age. All this, I hope, is a thing of the past. Although we do have teeth scalers in kennels, they are never used if a dog is fed the way I have described.

Over the many years that we have been rearing puppies we have tried many of the complete foods that have come on the market. I introduced one (an American product) in GDBA for the first time, and we fed it to a number of our brood bitches. We also reared their puppies on two very different products of this manufacture. The Labrador puppies made steady progress up to six weeks of age. The German Shepherd puppies did not do so well, nor did their dams. They appeared to be disinterested in the type of food and the puppies became emaciated. The problem with the product, and indeed with many other complete diets that we have tested, is that although young Labrador puppies did well when they were fed on it for a long period of time, many of them had difficulty in producing normal motions at regular intervals, which is essential in a puppy-walked dog. Pups were defecating on pavements while they were out for walks, a problem that also arose with dogs in training. Furthermore, the motions being passed were not well formed, but the type we describe as pancakes and anal gland problems became more prevalent. While we were still trying these products our trainers reported that they had been accused of turning Leamington pavements into a skid pan. You will not be surprised to learn that we no longer use complete foods.

Another problem that rose with dogs fed on soft diets was coprophagia (eating excrement) because the motions are still palatable. It is not generally a problem with dogs fed on what I term hard-tack (good roughage), and I have found that the cure is to switch to a diet such as raw meat on the bone, breasts of mutton or sheep's heads. Alternatively, add one or two dessertspoons of sterilised bone flour to the meal for a dog the size of a Labrador. Dry wheatmeal biscuit and hard raw bone will also ensure that the dog's motions do not taste very nice. However, I must emphasise that this is only a cure if the animal is kept on 'hard-tack', and is not run with other dogs given soft feeding (such as canned food), otherwise the motions of their kennel mates will be quite palatable. When a dog is fed on hard roughage its motions are not attractive to him or his mates. One word of caution. Rough feeding should only be used on medium to large breeds once they have received their adult teeth. On no account should it be given to a young dog or to an older dog who has never experienced it before.

Not long ago I heard a very instructive talk by a dentist, who has practised animal as well as human dentistry. His experience with tigers, hippopotami and numerous other species showed that while they rarely had dental problems in the wild, in captivity their teeth often decayed and infection set in, because they were not being able to clean or scale their teeth with the foodstuffs they were given by their human captors. The result was much suffering, and the dentist was regularly called in to put things right. All this could have been prevented had a study of the animals' natural feeding habits been carried out. I talked with him afterwards, and I was pleased to hear that he fully approved of hard feeding as a means of keeping mouths and alimentary systems healthy.

Most people who rear young dogs take the view that additives to the diet are beneficial, especially with the larger dogs. We have used a variety of mineral and vitamin supplements over the years. Cod-liver oil has been used in huge quantities, at one time we had it delivered in 25 gallon drums which went down very quickly. We also gave calcium tables because in the early sixties quite a high percentage of our puppies developed foreleg lameness, often when they were only five months old. We progressed, on veterinary advice, to feeding such products as Vivamin, Vitalyn, Vionate, SA37, Stress and sterilised boneflour, all in the hope that we would produce better puppies that were not afflicted with sore front legs. At no stage were we ever advised against feeding such products, quite the reverse in fact. It was always "give a little more", or "try this other product".

We then changed from cod-liver oil to halibut oil, in capsule form rather than by the spoonful, in order to control the amount being taken by the youngster. We still had pups that limped and this problem persisted for twenty five-years or more. I have researched the condition as far afield as Finland, Sweden, the USA and Australia, and I realised we were not alone in being troubled by this problem. Then, I realised that although we had changed our products and supplements, we had never tried rearing puppies on a natural diet without any kind of supplement, which is what would happen in nature. Although I still believe that certain puppies benefit from having supplements in their diets, it is very difficult to assess how much of each product is needed and how long a period to feed it. Rearing puppies successfully is very much a balancing act and each pup requires to be assessed individually.

At the breeding and puppy unit based at Tollgate House we ran an experiment over three years to assess if supplements did affect limping puppies. We had four puppy-walking supervisors, each with a different area. Every year supervisors placed seventy to seventy-five puppies in the homes of walkers and the litters were generally distributed around all the areas. The breeds were our standard stock, namely Labradors, Golden Retrievers, crosses of these two breeds, German Shepherds, some Collies, Curly Coats and Curly Coat crosses – all breeds which grow to a reasonable size quite quickly. The results were as follows:

FIRST GROUP

The puppies were placed on full supplements in the form of halibut oil capsules and sterilised bonemeal. This group produced the highest percentage of puppies with foreleg limp, commencing in most cases at five months of age and persisting right through to maturity when, in most cases, the limp disappeared. Some required surgery either on the elbow or shoulder, and in others the limp disappeared between seven and nine months of age, even though they were still on the supplements. (Nine out of seventy limped at some stage.)

SECOND GROUP

The second batch of seventy were fed supplements of halibut oil only, and had a very much reduced incidence of the limp, even though the progeny were from similar or the same litters as the first lot. (Three out of seventy limped at some stage – finally all came right.)

THIRD GROUP

The third batch were fed bonemeal supplement only, and again had a reduced incidence of limpers. (Two out of seventy-three.)

FOURTH GROUP

This group was fed on a natural diet with no supplements whatsoever, and produced NO limping puppies. It was the first year ever that we had this number of puppies with no limpers among them, and this seemed to imply that over-supplementation might be the root of our trouble.

The same experiment was carried out a second year and a third year, and although the picture was not quite the same, the results of all three years showed that the puppies fed on both supplements (halibut oil and bonemeal) always included a significantly higher proportion of limping puppies. Foreleg limp puppies were usually ones that were good convertors, with good bone strength. In most cases they were large-framed puppies that had grown quickly. The exercise led us to be cautious of over-supplementation, and we now use supplements to diet in a very limited way.

Food intake should be related to energy requirements, and for the average dog about 20 per cent of the calories should come from protein. In the case of lactating bitches or working dogs this proportion should be at least 22-25 per cent. Good quality commercial dog foods have a minimum of 22-28 per cent quality protein on a dry-matter basis. A dog utilises carbohydrates with almost the same efficiency as a human. They are economical sources of energy and help spare the proteins from being used as energy. In fact, carbohydrates can supply 60 per cent of dietary calories. Raw starches are generally rather poorly digested and are cooked during the processing of commercial dog food.

Chapter Fourteen

IDENTIFYING AILMENTS

Anyone looking through a veterinary textbook on canine ailments might well wonder how so many dogs live to a ripe old age. To list all the conditions and diseases that a dog may suffer from would be an impossible task, but I have picked out some which I think are of particular interest. Others I have dealt with in previous chapters.

HIP DYSPLASIA (HD)

Of all the conditions afflicting the dog, this is the one that causes most heartache, and keeps the printing presses of the dog world in business. Until 1960-61 canine HD was not generally recognised as a real problem. Cases had been seen and articles had been written on the subject by eminent vets, including G. D. Schenelle, but it was not until the sixties that we, at GDBA, encountered our first severely affected case. It occurred in a German Shepherd Dog puppy named Ishka, who was being walked in the Surrey area. She had all the classic physical signs of a badly afflicted HD puppy: very loose hind action carp back, lack of hind thrust and propulsion, and high and protruding crests area (croup and sacrum). These symptoms were accompanied by difficulty in achieving a normal, tight and tidy sitting position – she sat frog-legged. Crepitus and slight pain were also evident, particularly when she rose from the lying down position and when she moved. She seemed to be very aware that something was wrong with her rear end, for when she was walking at a normal speed, or gaiting fast, she either paced or bunny-hopped. X-rays showed that she had gross HD, with the femoral heads attempting to remodel themselves, and curvature of the femoral long bones. Ishka was six to seven months of age, and the prognosis was that she would rapidly deteriorate. Arthritis would set in as cavities filled, and life expectancy would be as short as two to three years. The vet recommended euthanasia.

At the time of this event, investigations by veterinary establishments had revealed that many dogs and bitches in the country were afflicted, particularly the giant or large breeds of dogs, and the incidence of breed-related affliction was reported to be as high as 60-70 per cent. Among the breeds afflicted were the Golden Retriever, the Labrador and the German Shepherd. It could be displayed in both sexes in the unilateral or bilateral form – in other words, in one or both hind legs.

The picture that emerged in the early sixties came as a great shock, and we were very concerned about the disastrous effect it could have on our dogs. In order to tackle the problem and prevent breeders using tainted stock, a scheme was proposed by the British Veterinary Association (BVA) whereby dogs and bitches could be X-rayed to determine whether they were afflicted. These X-rays could be assessed, for a fee, by a leading panel of veterinary radiology specialists and, if clear, a certificate of normality would be issued. This was originally known as the Canine Hip Dysplasia Eradication Scheme, but the name was later changed to the Hip Dysplasia Evaluation Scheme. It became evident that there was only a limited number of clear stock in certain breeds, and eventually it became necessary to issue 'Breeders Letters', in addition to certificates of normality, which indicated that although the animal in question was not completely clear, it was not markedly afflicted.

The problem was thought to be solely genetic in origin, so the scheme of certification could only guarantee that the animal in question was free of hip dysplasia on an X-ray; it did not guarantee that the animal was genetically free. Most were not, as we found out, but it was the only sure way of determining hip state in the living dog. In my view, this remains the only accurate way to diagnose hip dysplasia – far too many rash diagnoses have been made on the basis of physical signs alone. At this time, many papers and articles were being written on the subject suggesting genetic origins for the condition. Hip dysplasia was claimed to be caused by recessive genes, dominant genes, irregular dominant genes with incomplete penetration, polygenic and multifactural. This was all very confusing. The only available advice was to X-ray, not to breed from a slightly afflicted dog, and to put down dogs that were afflicted to a moderate or serious degree. This left a lot to be desired, because we had to meet the needs of three training centres, with a fourth centre on the way, all with long waiting lists of visually handicapped clients wishing to have a guide dog. In addition, we needed to establish a breeding force of animals which would have many desirable qualities to pass on to their progeny, but none of the undesirable hereditary traits, such as PRA, cataracts, epilepsy, heart defects and skeletal defects. With hindsight, the impracticality of the advice is now clearly evident. At the time only three German Shepherd breed champions held certificates of normality, and none of these had the temperamental characteristics or performance ratings suitable for producing guide dogs. Using these dogs to improve the hip state would have prevented the development of many other vital qualities and would, in effect, have been throwing the baby out with the bath water.

We X-rayed most puppy-walked dogs and stock coming in from outside, and we were getting progressively more confused. Many different views were expressed by different vets, including our own practice. I discussed the problem with Dr. G. Brookes, who looked after my own dogs and had a lot of experience with radiography. His advice, on seeing the many X-rays and hearing the decisions made on stock, was, and still is, the most practical advice I have heard on the subject. It helped to clear my own mind and came, free of charge, at a time when we were throwing many good dogs on the scrap heap, yet keeping their brothers and sisters with good hips on X-ray but perhaps weaker in character and temperament. The procedure we eventually adopted was to assess puppies and outside dogs on functional traits, and X-ray only if a problem was evident. If dogs and bitches were shown to be capable of regular daily walking, could sit, lie down and rise, cope with steps, jump easily in and out of the vehicles without discomfort and maintain tension on the lead they would be submitted for training. We did not expect all dogs to have perfect, or near-perfect movement. Providing they moved freely, and were capable of sustaining a regular and required speed for a reasonable period of time, they were accepted. We standardised and centralised X-rays and advice on HD through one reliable veterinary source, insisting that the X-rays were of good quality and that the animal was positioned for X-rays in an approved manner. All potential breeding stock was X-rayed, again relying on one reliable vet, and we retained animals with the best hips, bearing in mind the other qualities that were needed. This policy has been followed for many years at the Breeding Centre and has been successful in allowing us to expand the breeding force to its present size and standard. Together with our own designed grading system, now over twenty-three years old, it has allowed growth with minimum wastage without reducing the average working life of the trained guide dog. In fact, working life has increased. The old BVA scheme has now been largely abandoned, or re-designed in favour of the scoring system. Our system, which has given GDBA the opportunity to expand and develop, should be written in tablets of stone and be issued to all who dispense information on proven methods and procedure.

The difficulty with HD is that many of the characteristics, which are typical of some dysplastic dogs, are also evident in animals whose hips show up as normal on the X-ray. This could lead the uninitiated to conclude that any dog with a wide gait or rolling action is dysplastic, and that a dog that is reluctant to sit may be in pain through HD, when he may be unable to understand the exercise. In the late sixties GDBA devised its own grading system, using our own vet. The past two decades of assessment and selection of stock have provided records and statistics which are both revealing and invaluable. They are a vital signpost for leading us away from trouble and alerting us to problems. Over the years we have bred, placed and trained thousands of dogs as guides, yet there have been very few grossly afflicted with HD. We are currently caring for almost 4,000 guide dogs, plus breeding animals. All have been screened on functional traits and all breeding stock have been X-rayed and graded. Our records show a moderate incidence of HD in Golden Retrievers, Labradors, German Shepherds, Curly Coat Retrievers and the cross breeds, yet in twenty-two years the number of guide dogs having to finish work because of the condition is only twenty-four, which represents 0.4 per cent rejection rate from a total of 5,415 dogs that finished work over that time. If you take into account the fact that the average working life has also increased slightly, the system, with all its imperfections and complications, has given a good return.

HD is still thought to be genetic in origin and inherited, although the mode of inheritance has still not been proved. It is also thought to be affected, to a degree, by environmental factors, for all puppies are thought to be born with normal hips. Weight gain, exercise, and stresses on joints in the early puppy stage may have a bearing on the final hip state.

The bitch Ishka mentioned earlier was returned to the puppy walker and lived a normal life. She required no veterinary attention, took normal exercise and eventually died of heart failure at the grand age of thirteen years.

Some years ago a woman called on me at our Breeding Centre in the hope that I would be able to give her some advice about the dog that she had at home, a big Labrador male of about six years of age. She told me that the dog had been diagnosed as having HD by a local vet, and she had been informed that it would probably become a cripple and so it should be put to sleep as soon as possible. She was thoroughly upset, and neither she nor her husband wanted to have the dog put down. However, over the weekend the woman had been into a local pub where the landlady had a daughter who worked for us at the Breeding Centre. The landlady heard the tale of woe about the dog and told her that we bred from dogs with HD – an unfortunate, but certainly a true statement, for in order to provide dogs for training in large numbers and with the many desired qualities we had to do this, but all breeding stock had the best grading in this respect.

I asked if the vet had examined the dog's movements prior to X-ray to confirm the limp was in the rear quarters. The answer was 'no'. I then asked her other questions and some of the answers suggested that the dog could be limping on the front leg rather than the back. As she lived locally and was still rather upset and did not have transport, I offered to take her home in my car, and on the way back she asked if I would take a look at the dog. When I saw the dog run up and down the lawn, I was in no doubt that the limp was very much on the right fore leg, and nothing to do with HD. By now I had established that the dog was not always under the owner's surveillance, and that just prior to his limp appearing he had been away for two or three days, possibly chasing bitches around the village green. I said he could well have been hit by a car, bumped himself in some other way, or even broken a claw. Perhaps his pads were rather sore. Many things could have happened.

I then asked the owner to hold the dog. Although he was a strong, vigorous and excitable lad, he did finally calm down, but he wasn't particularly happy about me handling his fore leg, and I got a full view of forty-two teeth, which warned me not to push him or my luck too far. Eventually I decided to tape his muzzle, and then I tried his fore leg for pain, twisting the pastern, checking the claws and toes and making sure none were broken, pushing his leg back, extending it and flexing it. The dog showed no real sign of pain until I rubbed the palm of my hand across the surface of his pads. He almost hit the roof, rearing up and growling like mad. When I was able to look closely I found a very large foreign body in the main pad of his front claw. After reassuring him, we put his bottom against the corner of a building and I asked the owner to stride across and grip him, so that with myself there, escape was difficult. Then, with a good pair of tweezers, I extracted a blackthorn that was about 5/8 inches in length. The dog immediately gained a new lease of life, shot round the garden and then came back to his mistress, and even to me, making a great fuss of us both. That was the end of his HD.

YEAR	NUMBER WORKING GUIDE DOGS	NUMBER FINISHED WORK	NUMBER FINISHED FOR HEALTH	PER CENT	P.R.A.	H.D.	CATARACTS	EPILEPSY AND FITS
1963/64		101	14	13.8	3	-	-	-
1964/65		101	10	9.9	-	-	-	-
1965/66		106	12	11.3	1	1	-	2
1966/67	1247	106	14	13.2	2	1	-	-
1967/68	1344	127	21	17.6	6	-	-	-
1968/69	1466	171	30	17.5	2	1	-	-
1969/70	1586	160	23	14.3	2	-	-	-
1970/71	1698	198	24	12.1	4	-	-	-
1971/72	1793	210	32	15.2	-	-	-	-
1972/73	1869	228	26	11.4	-	-	-	-
1973/74	1984	220	32	14.5	3	-	3	2
1974/75	2122	263	47	17.8	4	2	1	1
1975/76	2269	267	32	11.9	2	-	-	-
1976/77	2373	291	28	9.6	1	2	1	3
1977/78	2537	255	68	25.4	4	1	-	2
1978/79	2630	329	54	16.4	1	1	4	3
1979/80	2777	406	51	12.5	2	4	2	1
1980/81	2931	362	92	25.4	2	4	9	3
1981/82	3109	337	57	15.1	2	3	6	3
1982/83	3254	410	94	22.9	2	1	6	3
1983/84	3489	378	70	18.5	2	2	7	5
1985	3602	349	50	14.3	2	1	5	3
	Total 5,415	Total 881			Total 46	Total 24	Total 42	Total 32

Percentage of total number finished work rejected for health = 16.2 per cent
"   P.R.A. = .8 per cent
"   H.D. = .4 per cent
"   Cataracts = .7 per cent
"   Epilepsy & Fits = .5 per cent
"   OCD = .0 per cent

FITS

The dog's nervous system, like that of humans, is very complex and any dysfunction, no matter how slight, is quickly manifested. Some of the most frightening manifestations are the various sorts of fits which affect dogs of all ages. They may occur as very mild tremors, but when seen as convulsions, they are usually associated with the dog kicking, frothing at the mouth, and in the more extreme cases becoming unconscious. The fit may last only a few seconds and occur when the dog is sleeping or just waking. The main cause is epilepsy, but what brings it on is, in many instances, difficult to pinpoint.

Fits can occur when puppies are cutting their teeth, especially if they are heavily infested with round or tape worms. They can also be triggered by shock, fear, injuries, stress, loud noises, sexual excitement or pain. I have even known large feeds, sudden changes in temperature or humidity, such as electrical storms, to set off an attack. The most difficult and persistent epileptic fits to treat often appear to have no specific trigger. They may be hereditary, the result of brain damage or of nerve damage after distemper, or possibly a result of encephalitis.

Because very little is understood of the problem it is essential to try to establish what triggers a fit. By the end of my career with GDBA, I had a thick file on dogs which had had fits, not all GDBA-owned. In the late sixties we had a spate of working guide dogs and puppies having fits, and all the afflicted animals were despatched to a clinic in London where the electrical activity of their brains was measured with an electroencephalograph (EEG). We decided in the end that the fit-epidemic was mainly triggered by electrical storms which had been sweeping across a belt of country where the majority of affected puppies lived. None of the pups concerned was of high breeding and none was sound-shy, so thunder did not worry them.

Many of the fitting puppies were rejected, but a small percentage was kept, on the vet's advice. Those that we did not reject, we were able to monitor and many of them went through life without further fits, although a few were given medication at the early signs of an electrical storm. It is interesting to note that many dogs with a predisposition to fits brought on by a storm appear to have an early warning system which their owners learn to recognise. One of our stud dogs was also caught up in this phase of fits. The dog was some six years of age when he had his first fit and it was eventually established that they were caused by encephalitis, which is not hereditary.

Many of the cases of fits that I have seen have been triggered by stress or anxiety. One incident I recall involved a Labrador bitch, owned by a publican who collected money for us. This bitch lived with him at the pub and regularly had fits during the first six or seven years of its life. It was on medication in the form of Mysolin. One day the owner said that he thought he might have found the cause of his dog's fits. I was sceptical, thinking that the animal was just having a long period between fits. However, he told me that he had an outsales department selling sweets, and every day he bought his bitch a half pound bar of bitter chocolate, which he gave her during the morning. At night she was again treated to bars of chocolate by the customers. Needless to say, the bitch became enormously overweight, and he therefore decided to cut out the chocolate. The bitch appeared to have stopped having fits, so he decided that the chocolate should be permanently withheld. The result was that the bitch lived to be fourteen years of age without having another fit. Some time later a leading neurologist told me it was quite feasible that the chocolate was a triggering factor.

One of the strangest experiences I had was with a group of good, healthy puppies that was placed on the puppy-walking scheme. When they were five or six months of age, I visited one, whose name was Ulan, in Harrogate. The puppy walker had walked pups for us in the past, and the supervisor thought I would be very pleased with this particular puppy. It was living with a couple and their three young daughters, who obviously adored him. When I arrived and the door was opened, the dog came bouncing up wagging his tail, obviously responding to the voice of the supervisor, who was with me and knew the dog well. About two yards from the door the dog saw me and suddenly put his brakes on. His tail went down, he barked furiously, then turned tail and shot back into the kitchen, urinating and showing all the symptoms of being very distressed. At first we thought he had been stung or had trodden on something that had hurt him, because the scene we had witnessed was very out of character with the dog's normal reaction to people, male or female. We went into the kitchen to find the dog cringing under the table, obviously very distraught. I bent down to comfort him, and he immediately urinated, trembling profusely and growling. It was obviously my presence that had disturbed him. I therefore asked the supervisor and the puppy walker to reassure him, put the lead on and get him out from under the table while I retired out of sight. They duly did this, but at no time while we sat and had a cup of tea would the dog relax. I asked the usual questions, such as "Does he normally show any signs of worry about males, particularly if they are dominant with animals?" – but the answer was no. He loved everyone and this incident was quite unexpected and obviously very distressing to the puppy walker.

After a while we took him out of the house for a short walk, and I asked the supervisor to take him ahead on the lead. I followed at some distance and noted that the puppy was quite relaxed and walked well. But as soon as I got close to them, the puppy's tail went down. He began to get tense and wanted desperately to get away to increase his own area of independence. I did eventually take over the lead, but at no time could I get the puppy to settle. After some thought I decided to take him back to Leamington for further investigation, assuring the puppy walker that we would do everything possible to overcome the problem. I got him back to the kennels and allowed him to settle down for a couple of days, asking the kennel staff to walk him, which they did without encountering any problems. He seemed to be an entirely confident and normal dog.

On the third day I presented myself in front of his kennel, intending to take him out for a walk. The two unrelated inmates in his kennel reacted as normal dogs, dancing at the gate and wanting to know me, hoping to be first out and to be going for a pleasant walk. Poor Ulan immediately reacted adversely, just as he did in the puppy walker's house, urinating all over the floor and bed and trying to get away through the French window opposite and out into the run. I managed to get him on the lead after sitting for a long time on the bed in his kennel reassuring him, and I walked him on several occasions, but at no time could I get him to relax. Yet my assistant, who regularly walked dogs from the kennels, was getting good walks from him. (My assistant, incidentally, was totally ignorant of the problems I was experiencing with the dog, which was not unusual, because we wanted independent, unbiased reports that were not tainted by other views). Two weeks after having him back, I was walking up the front of the kennels when I noticed one of the female supervisors walking a very nice-looking pale Labrador that I immediately recognised as Ulan. He was approaching me through the arch and when we were about 20 yards apart, he suddenly panicked and reacted in the usual way, spinning the supervisor round and desperately trying to escape. I caught up with them, and as we stood talking the dog continued to show signs of distress and had to be reassured by the handler. She asked what on earth I had been doing to the dog, and I replied that I hadn't done anything to Ulan. To my surprise she told me that the dog at her side was not Ulan, but Uffa, his brother.

I decided to have the whole litter in for assessment. There were two bitches and four dogs, and the outcome was that the bitches were perfectly alright with me, and so was one black male, but the other yellow brother, Ulla, reacted in the same way as the two original yellow dogs. We thought at first that they were reacting to a dominant handler, because they all were OK with other males they met. While all this was going on we were visited by members of the Metropolitan Police Dog Section. All of the litter seemed perfectly happy with them, but when I made my way down to the kennels, tiptoed round the back of the handlers and made my way to the front, the reaction was catastrophic. The three yellow brothers went up the wall – they urinated and two of them yelled to get out of the kennel. The black brother stood at the gate wagging his tail. The dog handlers present were totally mesmerised by the reaction that my presence had triggered off. I neither spoke to the dogs nor made any attempt to pat them, and I was particularly careful not to look directly at any particular one. Yet the reaction from all three was immediate. Something seemed very wrong, so we decided to send them for an EEG test in London.

The tests were done while I was holding the dogs, and the results showed that the three dogs who reacted so badly in my presence all had a predisposition to epileptic fits. They therefore had to be rejected and were placed in homes as pets, with the owners being fully informed as to why we had rejected them. They all lived to a good age and none of them ever had a fit or a similar reaction. The three that did not react adversely to me had normal EEGs and went on to train as guide dogs.

To this day I am perplexed as to why three dogs from a litter of six should react in the way they did, although the tests did indicate abnormal electrical activity in their brains. The incident also shows that there is more to the dog than ever meets the eye.

OSTEOCHONDROSIS DISSECANS (OCD)

This condition is not a great problem among guide dogs, but we are currently sponsoring a research programme on it in conjunction with the Royal Veterinary College. OCD came into prominence in the sixties when many of the bigger breeds became fashionable. It was then noticed that foreleg lameness was a problem in young dogs of five to six months of age. As Dalmatians were among the first in which it was noticed, the condition became known as Dalmatians' disease for a short time.

The dogs first developed a lameness which became progressive and painful when the shoulder joint was extended. There was also some atrophy, which is a failure to develop in the shoulder, and evidence of crepitus, which is grating. In 1968 four times as many male dogs as females had this condition, although, curiously, since 1980 the ratio is down to 2:1. One obvious question is whether it is caused by a difference in the way males and females grow. Although originally known as Dalmatians' disease, it is now clearly seen as a general condition in breeds with a body weight in excess of 50lbs, with the exception of Border Collies, particularly those used for obedience and agility work.

Most of the good advice that I have received on this condition has been from Gary Clayton Jones, BSc. FRCVS. He first became interested in the problem in 1965, having read a paper about the condition. OCD in the shoulder joint begins to show at a time when bone growth is rapid, which is about four to six months of age. The key to diagnosis is an X-ray, with the dog lying on its side. The vet looks for a change in the substance of the head of the humerus, particularly in the posterior third, which is usually the place to find OCD.

Inflammation in the joint, caused by a breakdown of cartilage, can cause secondary problems while the inflammation is present. Fragments, called ossicles, sometimes referred to as 'joint mice', break off, after which the lameness tends to improve. Usually it does not return, although on an X-ray the ulcer where the fragments came from can be seen. Fragments can be covered over by cartilage and the dog may not be lame, but just restricted in shoulder movement. To get fragments away, exercise has been tried, but most people cannot accept the amount of lameness and pain that a dog has to endure before the fragments break off. The best treatment is to remove the fragments surgically and allow cartilage to repair the gap where they have been broken off. Dogs can become lame, even when the fragment has not broken off and is just a crack, when fat or fluid get underneath and cause pain. X-rays will also reveal changes in the substance of the bone, and the surface can be seen becoming flattened off, with evidence of small holes, some even becoming cavities.

It has been suggested that something goes wrong where the change from cartilage to bone takes place that allows fragments to become loose. It is also possible that something in the sex hormones causes changes or that one joint is damaged as a result of injury. Hereditary factors may have some bearing.

OCD can be seen in joints other than the shoulder. It occurs, again mainly in larger breeds, in the stifle (the middle joint of the leg), the elbow and the hock (which corresponds to the human ankle). The signs are the same, starting when the puppy is about five months or so. It can easily be mistaken for hip dysplasia and an X-ray can confirm a degree of hip dysplasia, but other symptoms may be different. The hock joint may show a little distention, or swelling may be seen just behind the tibia, although this may be concealed in the longer-coated breeds. In the hock, a fragment of cartilage from the edge can become loose and remain in place, staying attached to the joint capsule. This can only be seen on an X-ray. It may cause some secondary arthritis and occasionally comes away and floats off into the back of the joint. The fragment can be removed, but surgery is not as successful as with the shoulder. Often the dog is no better than it was before the operation.

In the elbow joint, OCD causes front leg lameness and pain, limited movement and possibly some inflammation that is visible on the inner side of the elbow. As before, it is mainly the larger breeds that are affected. OCD covers various joint problems, including ununited coronoid process, which particularly affects the Golden Retriever and the Labrador. Dogs can have OCD and ununited coronoid together. Normally surgery is recommended for persistent lameness, but it is usually more successful in the shoulder than in the hock or the elbow. Coronoid processes can cause a great deal of rubbing of the bone and epicondial grooving and bone fragments can be found. It is best to wait until the dog is seven to eight months old before deciding to operate. To take a dog off one leg when it is young can cause stress to be placed on the other legs, with resulting problems. There is also a possibility that the condition may improve itself with rest and not need surgery at all, so it is often difficult to know what is the best course of action to take. Our experience is that without surgery 80 per cent come right, but keeping them on a correct diet and correct body weight, with limited exercise, is important.

Of all the difficulties that we have encountered with puppies over the last twenty-eight years, foreleg limp has been the biggest. Usually puppies begin limping at five months of age, some being affected in both legs. Initially we had no idea what the cause was and much research, endeavour and money was spent on veterinary investigation and treatment. X-rays, though costly, were regularly taken on afflicted stock, yet they rarely showed why the pup should be so lame. I discussed the problem with the guide dog schools in the United States, Australia and New Zealand. All were aware of the problem, but none had come up with the cause or with any effective treatment. Experience generally showed that 80 per cent would grow through the limping stage and become sound at nine to eleven months of age, depending on breed, yet 20 per cent were afflicted for life. If only we could have sifted those 20 per cent out at six weeks of age – but at that stage they were all as good and sound as each other.

As with HD we had a flood of differing advice from the veterinary profession up and down the country, usually to the effect that the pup was deficient in some mineral or vitamin (yet we had always fed supplements to diet). Another opinion that we encountered regularly was that the animals were in-bred and that we were making our own problems. As time would eventually tell, neither of these hypotheses was accurate. Over the years we had used most, if not all, the different supplements on the market, always on veterinary advice: products such as calcium tablets, powdered calcium, vitamins A & C & D, Vionate, Vivo Min, Stress S.A.37, bonemeal, cod-liver oil, halibut-liver oil and many other products, none of which ever made any real difference to the problem. In 1982-83 I decided to run a controlled experiment on puppies, and the results of this are detailed in the Chapter on Health and Nutrition. However, it is interesting to note that of the four groups on different diets, the one that was fed no supplements (bonemeal or halibut oil) consistently produced fewer limping puppies.

There is now no doubt in my mind that rapidly growing pups of large frame are more prone to OCD than others. These puppies are, in most cases, produced by parents who are typical of the breeding, and one is therefore inclined to link the OCD to hereditary factors. This could be so, but I believe that the main factor is the balanced rearing of the puppy during its critical physical development period. Our controlled experiment showed how easily the balance can be upset – and particularly in puppies, such as ours, where regular exercise is necessary in order to expose the pup to external influences at the critical stages of its development.

A final word should be said on the symptoms of OCD compared with those of hip dysplasia. The hip joint is a ball and socket type and in all breeds some animals will show defects in this area. One or other part of the joint can be the wrong shape, or tissue may lapse, the resulting condition being called HD. It was decided a long time ago that this was an hereditary disease, and in the sixties it became fashionable to X-ray dogs before using them for breeding. It has been said that a dog with HD will grow up to have severe arthritis and may even become paralysed. In a dog with HD, the ball and socket rub against each other, causing thickening of the capsule of the joint. There may be some wearing away on the two surfaces of the cartilage, which may become dust, and some fluid may appear within the joint. If this is excessive, inflammation may occur, causing the dog to cry because of the pain, particularly if the lining of the joint, where the nerves are present, is affected. In HD the socket will flatten off and the head will expand until the gap is closed again.

The resulting condition is called osteo-arthritis, and if monitored through the rest of the dog's life, it will be seen to stabilise, although the joints may be deformed. It may be seen in puppies, when again the inflammation occurs, but it then disappears and the dog becomes sound, staying this way for the rest of its life. There may be some restrictions on extension of the limbs, but the dog will be quite happy and free from pain. The majority of dogs picked at random will have a degree of HD, but pain could well be from OCD in the hock. Both conditions have similar symptoms, and Mr Clayton Jones does not place too much emphasis on HD. Even severe conditions at six months may improve, with the dog becoming fairly sound. Pet dogs and, in some cases, guide dogs will remain capable of work and are quite healthy. Service dogs or police dogs with HD will not be able to endure the work required of them, as they are involved with vertical board scrambling and negotiating obstacles that may need them to flex their hip joints. The dog walking at a moderate pace, as the guide dog generally does, does not need to flex its hips.

1980/1982 SURVEY ON O.C.D. PUPPIES

Puppies placed on Tollgate's Scheme	595
GDBA Bred	550 *
Acquired from outside sources	45 *
Number of pups (both groups) with identified and unidentified limps	38
Number of GDBA bred pups with identified and unidentified limps	33
Number of outside bred pups with identified and unidentified limps	5

Therefore, 33 of 550 GDBA bred = 6 per cent.   Therefore, 5 of 45 outside stock = 11.1 per cent

Rejected = 3 = **.5 per cent**   Rejected GDBA Bred = 2 = **.3 per cent**   Rejected Outside Bred = 1 = **2.2 per cent**

*GDBA sample x 12 larger than outside breeding

BREAKDOWN OF BREEDS

No. PLACED	No LIMPING	PER CENT	AT WALK	REJECTED	TRAINING	QUALIFIED
LABRADORS						
272	20	7.4	3	0	10	7
GERMAN SHEPHERDS						
87	10	11.5	2	3	3	2
G.RETRIEVER/X/LAB						
120	4	3.3	2	0	1	1
GOLDEN RETRIEVERS						
92	3	3.3	0	0	0	3
LAB/X/CC RETRIEVER						
11	1	9.1	1	0	0	0

NUMBER OF BREEDING ANIMALS CONNECTED WITH 38 PUPS WHICH DEVELOPED LIMPS

LABRADORS	272 placed	20 limping = 7.4 per cent
GERMAN SHEPHERDS	87 placed	10 limping = 11.5 per cent
G.R./X/L	120 placed	4 limping = 3.3 per cent
GOLDEN RETRIEVERS	92 placed	3 limping = 3.3 per cent
LAB/X/CCR	11 placed	1 limping = 9.1 per cent

OUTCOME OF THE 38 DOGS

14 In Training   **13** Qualified   **8** At Walk   **3** Rejected

Afflicted pups sired by: **14** Different GDBA stud dogs   **3** Different outside stud dogs

Out of: **28** GDBA brood bitches   **5** Different outside brood bitches   **5** Different breeds

CRYPTORCHID AND MONORCHID

The term monorchid is commonly used by dog people to describe male animals in which only one testicle has descended into the scrotum, the other testicle being retained in the abdomen. Such an animal is correctly called a unilateral cryptorchid. The term monorchid should be reserved for an animal with a single testicle, which is a far rarer condition. A bilateral cryptorchid is one that has both testicles retained in the abdomen. It is said that cryptorchidism is an inherited condition but the precise mechanisms of inheritance have not yet been determined.

Some years ago I arranged to do an exchange with a breeder in Suffolk. She desperately wanted a well-bred black Labrador male of ours and I was keen to obtain a yellow Labrador bitch from one of her bitch's litters. Our male was about eight weeks of age when she had him from us, and after a couple of weeks she rang me up saying that she felt a little disappointed because her vet had stated that he was a bilateral cryptorchid. This seemed rather remarkable, because we had checked him at the breeding centre, prior to parting with him, and found him to be entire with both testicles descended. However, I arranged to go down and see the puppy the following week. In the meantime, she rang up and said that a very well known and respected breeder of Labradors, who was a friend of hers, had checked the puppy and found him to be entire. On the day of my visit the vet had been in the morning and found that the puppy had only one testicle descended. I called in the afternoon and, sure enough, the puppy did appear to have only one testicle descended. I had another call to make and so arranged to return later to collect the puppy and find her another one. When I returned later in the afternoon to collect the puppy, she announced that the puppy was now entire. I checked and both its testicles were indeed in the scrotum. The puppy had the capacity, as some do, to retract the testicles if he is a little unsure on being handled. The dog stayed with her and sired several litters.

Breeding from bilaterial cryptorchids is not possible. With both testicles retained in the abdomen they are kept at a temperature that prevents the production of sperm – the dog is therefore infertile. Unilateral cryptorchids can be used because, of course, one testicle has descended and is being maintained at the right temperature in the scrotum, but it would be unwise to breed from such a dog in case the condition is passed on to the offspring.

SOFT EARS

Soft ears are not necessarily a veterinary problem, but it is an interesting condition.

It might appear in the German Shepherd where the young pup's ears either never go up, or perhaps go up for a little while and then flop down. It is not a serious condition but it can make the dog look a little odd.

German Shepherd puppies' ears are soft initially, and the age at which they become erect varies. Some puppies that manage to get their ears up can have a tendency to let them drop when they commence teething. If this happens, there is usually no need to worry, for they will go up again once the teeth have broken through. However, a puppy that has got well through the teething stage and still has ears that are semi-erect or floppy requires assistance. With this type of puppy the sooner something is done, the better. There are two methods of attempting to get the ears erect:–

1. Fold the ear in half vertically and tape around the extremities of it, leaving the tip untaped. Ideally, the procedure would be to go right down to the root so that the ear stands erect rather than flopping to one side, because the danger is that the taped ear will stand out to the side and the dog will look bat-eared.

2. This is the method that I recommend. Clean and shave the inside of the ear carefully, then cut a piece of chiropodist felt, possibly about 1/8 of an inch thick with adhesive backing, to the exact shape of the ear so that the felt drops flat inside the ear and down, with a stem into the ear canal itself. Press the felt firmly on the inside of the ear between your hands and then fold the ear edges together, A-B right ear, B-C left ear, and tape as before on the outside, leaving the tip untaped to allow a passage for air to get down the ear itself. This tape should stay on for a minimum of ten days. If both ears require treatment, then after taping the individual ears, arrange a brace across the back of the ears high up but below the little bit which is untaped. Normally, if this is done well, the ears of most puppies can be made to stand, unless they are lacking in muscle tone at the root. Ice-lolly sticks bound in tape make good bracing equipment.

Use will strengthen a puppy's ears. Walking it in the dark will encourage it to listen and thus strengthen the ear muscles. Another thing I believe in is the hard feeding of bones, to strengthen the masticatory muscles and the temporal muscles which run to the ear.

METRITIS

This is inflammation of the uterus and occurs after whelping. It appears to be caused by dead puppies, retention of an after-birth, injury or infection during whelping. We have had very little experience of this condition with our bitches, and I believe it can usually be avoided by good monitoring of a bitch during and after parturition and the rearing of a litter. We do not give all our bitches antibiotics after whelping, but strict hygiene and observation are maintained by kennel staff. Twice-daily checks are carried out on all nursing dams and any abnormalities are quickly reported to the veterinary surgeon. It is important to ensure all after-births have been expelled at the end of a birth. If in doubt, the veterinary surgeon should be called.

FALSE PREGNANCY

A bitch will exhibit all the signs of first stage labour by making beds, carrying toys about, etc. The udder fills up and often the milk will drip. If not treated, the symptoms may persist for a week or two. False pregnancy is seen in quite a number of bitches and occurs because they have been through the oestrus season stage and are mentally prepared for having puppies. I have known a bitch change her mode of barking to a very light protective bark if anyone goes near the place where she believes she has got her puppies. I have also known bitches nuzzle stones and clean them as they would puppies and convert certain areas in the house, such as a cupboard, where they imagine they have got litters.

One bitch that I owned myself always, at about six or seven weeks after season, dug a huge hole in the soil under the kennel and retired to her earth. No amount of persuasion, other than physical, would induce her to leave the spot and she was quite protective of it. Usually with bitches like this, the activity ends a week before normal: instead of extending to the ninth week, they normally go through their whelping phase a week earlier. If they have blown up and look to be in whelp (although their shape is normally more round than dropped) they usually return to normal in the eighth week. Even bitches which have been mated and missed may go through these symptoms and return to normal a week before normal whelping. Spayed guide dog bitches never have false pregnancies and so avoid the physical and mental upset of these hormone-dependent problems.

A word of warning here. Both with a bitch that is carrying and with others who are having a false pregnancy, keep a keen eye on their whereabouts. I have known settees to be ripped up and bedspreads destroyed when they have been chosen as nest areas for the impending litters. An anxious bitch is no respecter of soft furnishings.

PYOMETRA

This is pus in the uterus (womb) and is seen mainly in maiden bitches, usually later in life. There are two types, closed pyometra and open, the only difference being that a discharge, which may or may not be offensive, is seen in an open pyometra. The bitch generally goes off-colour, starts to drink excessively and might run a high temperature, although usually not. The only satisfactory treatment for the closed type is to spay the bitch, and if this is done prior to the toxic syndrome it is virtually 100 per cent successful. Where the bitch is toxic and vomiting, the success rate goes down. Delay in operating may mean a survival rate of 50 per cent or even less. The clear discharge variety can usually be dealt with and treated by the vet with antibiotics.

Many breeders believe that if a bitch is regularly bred from – say every other season if she is on a six month cycle, or every season if the cycle is ten months or a year – she will not develop pyometra. Very few of our brood bitches have had to have a pyometra operation, so there could well be something in the belief. My experience with older bitches is that where they have had a season which trails on for longer than normal, and discharges show signs of being dirty, pyometra is likely to develop. A number of these cases can be dealt with by medical treatment initially, but as each successive season comes round, the problem becomes worse and eventually a pyometra operation is needed.

WET ECZEMA

Perhaps the commonest form of this inflammation of the skin is acute moist eczema, which seems to be caused by excessive feeding of carbohydrates. Some people say that any dog fed exclusively on high carbohydrate foods like bread and potatoes will produce a moist eczema on the skin surface within a month.

A heavy infestation of fleas or lice can produce a raw patch, as also can acute stress or anxiety. The symptoms are violent biting and scratching of a localised area, and if you look closely you will see an acutely painful circular moist patch, often infected and scabbed over. A search of the area may reveal fleas or lice.

We don't hear as much of wet eczema nowadays as we used to. In the early sixties there were a lot of cases in the training centres, and it was found to be linked with the short training times and the demands this made on the dog. The usual treatment for it at that time was 'pink lotion' (calamine) which, when used sensibly by soaking it into the raw skin, did have a beneficial effect. If dogs are allowed to lick calamine lotion, however, they will often become sick. If a dog is suffering moist or wet eczema over the rump, down the side of the cheeks or at the back of the ears and cheeks, fleas are most likely to be the cause – they are, I believe the reason for a lot of skin troubles. Mosquito bites and other insect bites may cause the sort of moist eczema known in the USA as 'hot spots'!

DRY ECZEMA

This is one of the most difficult skin conditions to diagnose and treat. The cause is obscure, but it may be no coincidence that it is seen most commonly in pedigree dogs. There may, therefore, be a hereditary predisposition. Symptoms are persistent scratching, producing dry, scaly areas of baldness and maybe a reddening of the skin surface.

Dry eczema is one of the most stubborn types, and cases we have dealt with over the years have always been extremely difficult to clear. Such things as internal parasites and tape worms, causing the coat to be harsh, dry and brittle, can produce conditions in which bacteria thrive, thus causing the dog to scratch and giving it areas of dry eczema. The usual treatment is to worm the dog for internal parasites. If that is the cause, you will get a response within two to three weeks.

One of our dogs suffered from dry eczema for the best part of a year, and we saw most of the skin specialists in the country before discovering that it was suffering from a massive infestation of tape worm. Once the worm was eradicated, the dog's coat returned to normal and all the bare, dry patches disappeared. Thereafter he stayed in glorious condition, never having another patch of dry eczema on him for the remaining nine years of his life. Yet when he was at his worst he was diagnosed by different vets as having both types of mange, dry eczema, allergy and finally seborrhoea, the last diagnosis coming from a well-respected dermatologist who said the only cure was euthanasia. However, we brought the dog back to the centre and decided to worm him, just in case. We now have a pound jam-jar, brimfull of his tape worms on exhibition in our museum. I would advise anybody with a dog that has skin problems to check for worms.

Dry eczema may, of course, be linked to hereditary factors and such things as hormone levels, particularly with bitches prior to coming into season. I saw this with a young bitch that I owned who kept in first-class condition up to four or five weeks before coming into season, when her whole attitude changed and she began to come out in large areas of eczema. The condition persisted throughout her season up to about the time, when if mated, she would normally be parting with her puppies, and then she came back to normal again. That pattern persisted throughout her life until she was eight years old, when she was spayed. When the seasons stopped, so did her skin problem. She lived to be fourteen, and never had any further problems or treatment.

MANGE: SARCOPTIC MANGE

This is also known as common mange, and it is caused by the sarcoptes mange mite. The mite burrows into the surface layer of the skin and lays its eggs, which keep hatching out. This produces persistent scratching, with rough bare patches appearing at the elbows, stifles, around the ears and the eyeballs. If neglected, the lesions spread over the entire body and the animal loses condition rapidly, because it has great difficulty in relaxing. Sarcoptic mange is very contagious: an affected dog needs to be isolated, and its kennel should be cleaned with brushes that are not used elsewhere. Proper protective clothing should be worn by staff dealing with the dog, and care should be taken not to transmit the mite to other animals.

DERMODECTIC MANGE (FOLLLICULAR MANGE)

This is much more serious for the dog than the sarcoptic mange because the parasite buries itself more deeply in the skin and takes in with it a staphylococcus bacterium which produces the characteristic lesions. The lesions appear slowly at first, with little or no itching, and are common in quite young dogs of under a year old. Bare patches appear round the eyes and nose and on the legs and feet, and emit a peculiar characteristic smell. The surface of the lesion is usually tufted and reddened, with pustules at the base of the tufts. Sometimes the skin is merely thickened and flaking. Often, despite treatment, the patches seem to spread and the dog can become toxic and emaciated.

Mange is rare, but one or two of our puppies seem to have been affected. With one line of German Shepherds, one puppy from each litter was found to have pustules on the chin which were attributed to demodex, and it is now believed the disease is transmitted from the dam, when the pups are suckling. However, the line, which goes back twenty-eight years, is still with us and only two puppies have been affected. We have handled thousands of dogs now, and in the early days, with dogs coming in from all sorts of environments, it was a condition that we saw in dogs from unkempt areas and poor housing conditions. It does not usually occur in well-kept dogs.

OTODECTIC MANGE

This is caused by a mange mite called the Otedectes cyanotis which is picked up from other dogs or cats. It lives in the ear, where it lays its eggs in a burrow in the mucus membrane. The symptoms are rather like those described as canker, where the dog scratches, flaps the ears and shakes the head. Diagnosis is confirmed by finding the mite with an auroscope or in wax examined under the lower power of the microscope.

The condition can be seen regularly in dogs, particularly in kennels where there is a large moving population, and it can be quite stubborn to clear. Normally the dog scratches at the ear with its feet. Mites get on to the feet, then drop to the floor, where another dog can pick them up, scratch itself and become infected. Many a time a cat has transmitted mites to the dog, and if this is the case both animals should be treated.

RING WORM

This complaint is fairly common and is caused by fungi which live either on the surface of the skin or more often in the hairs of the affected areas. The first signs are scratching or biting at the skin, and an examination shows a rounded patch of crusty skin with hairs falling out.

The condition is not what it sounds to be. It certainly is not caused by a parasitic worm. It is fungal and the spores from the fungus are highly contagious. Over the years numerous cases of ring worm have been reported but when we have brought them in, isolated them, and had our vet check them, they were found not to be suffering from the disease. It appears that many skin conditions can be mis-diagnosed and are often thought to be ring worm. I have dealt with 30-40,000 dogs and have only seen about four cases.

SOFT PADS

When soft pads occur, look at the environment in which the dog is being worked or kept. In kennels, for example, the use of strong bleaches has on many occasions been the cause of pads that lack husk or protective cover and therefore become sore if the dog is walked regularly. Dogs that are constantly kept on wet surfaces also tend to have soft pads.

The ideal is, of course, to improve the accommodation by making sure the dogs are kept on dry surfaces and walked steadily until the protective layer has been encouraged to grow on the pad. Rock alum applied to the pads can assist the hardening, providing they are not blistered or broken. Surgical or methylated spirit can also help.